IT
TAKES
ALL
SORTS!

IT TAKES ALL SORTS!

ILLUSTRATED BY
FFOLKES

WRITTEN BY
JANE REID

OCTOPUS BOOKS

First published in 1984
This edition published in Great Britain in 1987 by

Octopus Books Limited
59 Grosvenor Street
London W1

Text and illustrations © 1984 Hennerwood
Publications Limited

ISBN 0 7064 2990 7

Printed and bound in the United Kingdom by
William Clowes Ltd, Beccles

CONTENTS

A Diet of Worms   7

Creators of Havoc   23

Mad Menagerie   37

The Aristocranks   51

There's Nowt as Queer as …   65

Driven to Distraction   87

Quirks of Passion   95

Extreme Cases   105

Strange Habits   119

Dead Odd   133

Creditable Cranks   145

A DIET OF WORMS

Consumers and preparers of extraordinary dishes.

Eggcentrics

Eccentricity can be the only explanation for the behaviour of many men and women who are so determined to have their names in the *Guinness Book of Records* that they stuff themselves with all sorts of odd foods.

Karen Stevenson of Wallasey in Cheshire, for example, gorged herself by eating 2,780 cold baked beans – one by one with a cocktail stick. It took her thirty minutes. That was twenty-two minutes longer than the time taken by David Barnes of Washington to eat 424 littleneck clams and more than twenty-nine minutes longer than it took Peter Dowdeswell to consume more than one pound of live elvers at Bristol in 1978.

This trio pale into insignificance when we think of another man whose name is inscribed in the Records Book for a feat that no one could ever want to emulate. It took Jay Gwaltney 89 hours to munch his way into history. If you think that is a long meal, consider that during that time he ate every last twig of an eleven-foot birch tree.

Lithophagropher Extraordinary

The word means stone swallower. (Yes! I had to look it up in a dictionary, too.)

One of the best known lithophagrophers of the nineteenth century was a foreigner who swallowed pebble after pebble in St George's Fields in London.

After he had eaten several, he would open his waistcoat and ask spectators to punch him in the stomach so that they could hear the rattling.

A Statue-Esque Policeman

Detective Inspector Eustace of the Metropolitan Police was famous for always getting his man, and went to extreme lengths to do so.

In the years before the First World War he disguised himself as a Fagin-like fence, complete with false nose, long wig and skull cap.

He dressed up as a woman many times (all in the line of duty, of course); but his devotion to duty was severely stretched one day when he posed on a pedestal for three hours in a convent chapel, hoping to catch an unsuspecting thief red-handed.

The relic robber was astounded when the long arm of the law appeared from nowhere and landed on his unsuspecting shoulder.

Making a Pig of Himself

The 'oohs' and 'aahs' of appreciation caused by the tantalizing smell of mouthwatering suckling pig coming from the kitchen, turned into gasps of astonishment when the animal was carried into the dining room on a vast silver platter borne by the butler.

The beast had been cooked to perfection. The crackling shone in the candlelight, but the sight of the butler with an apple in his mouth and herbs sprinkled over his coat was too much for the assembled guests, who included the Prime Minister, Mr Baldwin.

The confusion had been caused when the servant had asked the mistress of the house how suckling pig should be served. Lady Orford had replied, rather vaguely 'Oh, rather dressed up — you know, an apple in the mouth and parsley behind the ears.'

The batty butler had taken her literally at her word!

A Poor Judge of Taste

No one batted an eyelid in the court building canteen when the judge removed the ham from his sandwich and replaced it with his paper napkin.

A dash of salt and a little pepper with just a soupçon of mustard seasoned the paper to perfection, and the loony law-officer munched his lunch happily.

'The judge is a great favourite with all the canteen staff,' the catering supervisor smiled indulgently. 'He's always up to something unusual.'

Dinner with the Emperor

Noble Romans dreaded receiving invitations to one of the Emperor Alagabalus's banquets, but such was his power that they had to attend.

To say that the Emperor's sense of humour was eccentric is a bit like saying that Henry VIII was a faithful husband.

Sometimes the food was so perfectly glazed it shone in the candlelight like glass or ivory. Very often it *was* glass or ivory. On more than one occasion guests were amazed at the lightness of the pastry, and if the filling tasted dubious, more often than not it *was* — lion's dung.

Offal or awful, the Emperor watched as his reluctant guests forced the gruesome food down their throats.

Needless to say there were few tears shed when Alagabalus died at the tender age of seventeen — struck down by the guards who were employed to protect him.

Perhaps he'd asked them for lunch.

An Appropriate Name

The Earl of Masserene liked nothing better than eating out of doors, and when the fancy took him he ordered his servants to arrange a picnic — not in the beautiful grounds of his stately home, but on the roof among the chimneys.

His staff would clamber through the attics carrying the dining room furniture — the polished table, all the chairs and, of course, the silverware. The kitchen staff put the food on hoists and the butler pulled it up. But, no sooner had the first course been served, than the earl invariably changed his mind and ordered that the performance be carried out in reverse and the things taken inside again.

Perhaps his Christian name had something to do with it — *Clotworthy*.

Supper's Up

Friends grew accustomed to the speed with which the food disappeared from Jamie Duff's plate — into his pocket.

Jamie kept house for his elderly mother and usually dined with her. However, he was occasionally asked out by his best friend and his wife and such was the wit and warmth of Jamie's conversation that they didn't mind at all that, instead of eating his food, he simply stuffed his pockets with whatever was put in front of him.

They knew that as soon as the last course had been served, Jamie would ram it into his pocket and rush home to share the repulsive repast with his mother.

Have a Heart

Frank Buckland was dedicated to increasing Britain's food supply in the mid-nineteenth century. He was a founder member of the Society for the Acclimatisation of Animals in the United Kingdom and in 1862 was responsible for that society's annual dinner.

The menu catered for all tastes! There was kangaroo meat from Australia and trepang sea-slug from south-east Asia. The meal was so revolting that none of the members would eat it. Buckland was surprised. He had been contemplating giving his guests earwigs, but these were, he considered, a trifle bitter.

Buckland's favourite snack was crocodile with orange juice. During his days as a student at Oxford, he served mouse on toast to his fellow students and at one dinner party the *pièce de resistance* was a whole roast ostrich.

Buckland's friends became rather wary of accepting dinner invitations, but one loyal companion could always be relied on. One night when the two were at table, Buckland said, 'I have eaten many strange things in my life, but never before have I eaten the heart of a king.'

He removed the cover from a dish and there, smuggled out of France whence it had been plundered during the French Revolution, was the heart of Louis XIV. This was too much for the long-suffering friend, who left in disgust – yet surely no one could accuse poor Frank of *heartlessness*.

An Iron Constitution

Having already eaten 22,500 razor blades, a ton of glass, loads of cutlery, chains, nuts and bolts, a Yugoslav man set about his greatest challenge in December, 1969: a bus.

The Yugoslav Press Agency has not yet let us know if he's finished; one suspects, though, that he bit off more than he could chew.

What a Sauce

'A lavish host' would be an understatement if applied to one American billionaire. His private jets flew in truffles from Perigord, lobsters from Maine, salmon from Scotland – wherever there was a luxury food in season it was searched out and brought to *San Simeon*, his luxury mansion.

The food was cooked to perfection by an army of chefs, served on silver plates to the waiting guests seated around the vast, polished oak table.

Yet – extraordinary sight among such gourmet delights – on every side plate was a *paper* napkin and beside each guest a bottle of tomato ketchup!

Off His Rock-er

It was a special occasion, but even so!

The pudding that Sir John Irwin organized for a certain smart dinner party was a spun-sugar, scale model of the Rock of Gibraltar, complete with canons that fired sugar plums against the walls of the hill-top fortress.

It cost £1,500.

Bathfuls of Kernels

A well-known South American was so convinced that walnuts were the secret of long-life that he kept two baths in his luxurious mansion full of them. Whenever he felt peckish he went to the lavatory and helped himself to a handful or two.

The Ultimate Gravy Train . . .

was owned by the Maharaja of Gwalior.

It was made of solid gold and carried his food from the kitchens to his table along 250 feet of solid silver rails.

Inner Cleanliness

Doctors are trained to show no surprise at the odd tastes of their patients.

Mothers-to-be are especially prone to developing fads during their pregnancies, but one doctor did splutter disbelievingly into his stethoscope when the toothbrush saleswoman he was examining admitted to him that, yes, actually, she did like the odd tipple. Her usual was one pint of Dettol every day.

Muncheon Vouchers

'You're supposed to *buy* lunch with them,' the girls in the typing pool explained to the new office junior.

The attractive girl smiled and continued to eat her way through her monthly allocation of luncheon vouchers. The girls soon got used to her predilection for a diet of paper, and hid their boxes of paper tissues and their magazines, but reams of typing paper began to disappear and the girl was dismissed.

She managed to stifle her odd appetite while she trained as a nurse, but didn't last long in her first job in a maternity home.

She nibbled her way through 35 birth certificates during her first and last week there, and was lucky to be dismissed without being certified herself.

Hair of the Dog, Anyone?

An elderly English colonel, who was as crusty as his favourite port, despised the vogue for pre-dinner cocktails that swept England in the 1920s.

There was only one acceptable pre-dinner drink — sherry, but he did offer his guests his own cocktail — a dash of brandy, a slurp of grenadine and a generous amount of a secret, blue ingredient.

The whole concoction was shaken not stirred and served perfectly chilled. No one ever asked for a second, and the next time a guest came for dinner he or she was happy with a sherry.

The secret ingredient was methylated spirits.

A Stickler for Etiquette

During the fish course at an upper-class dinner party, a fish-bone became stuck in the throat of one man who was a proper stickler for etiquette.

He could never have embarrassed his hostess by coughing and spluttering — so instead he went quietly blue in the face and died.

A Suitable Prize

Roger Martinez entered a strange competition and won handsomely. His prize was a free fish dinner — an appropriate reward for having swallowed 225 live goldfish.

Quite a Mouthful

Customers in a Campbeltown bar were astonished when a sailor drained his glass of Scotch and then began to crunch the tumbler between his teeth.

The eccentric gastronome refused to pay for the glass and was thrown into the local gaol after the fight that ensued was broken up by the police.

When he was taken from his cell the next morning the officers were astonished to find that he had broken the window in his cell – with his teeth!

'I was feeling a bit peckish,' he explained to the sheriff who promptly fined him £10 . . . for wilful damage to police property.

Meals on Wheels

Guests at the home of Gaston Menier often complimented him on the quality of service at table. Not only was it fast and efficient, it was almost silent.

Menier had built a miniature electric railway which carried food from the kitchen directly on to the table. The host controlled the four-track system which carried the food-loaded carriages.

Fifty pounds of food could be carried at two miles an hour.

And on the Third Day, He Died

Everyone in southern Ireland had heard of Harry Badger. For, it was said, old Harry would eat anything.

A pint of thick black porter would slip down Harry's throat — he swallowed the dead mouse that was also in the glass with apparent unconcern. He didn't bat an eyelid at the plateful of potatoes and pebbles that was placed before him: he gulped them down his gruesome gullet.

Unfortunately, his gourmandising was his downfall in the end. The bowl of 'tripe' placed before him was really strips of boiled leather smothered in a milk and honey sauce. One day's constant munching made little impact either on Harry or the 'tripe'. He really got his teeth into it on the second day and almost finished it. He set about it with relish on the third day — but died before the plate was empty.

Too Near the Bone

Thomas Wallace was delighted when his wife became pregnant.
So was his 'little lady', until he developed an unusual plan to
ensure that their offspring would be born with strong, healthy
bones.

He made her eat bone-meal fertilizer every day for a month,
until she found it – and husband Tom – too hard to swallow and
left him.

What a Clot

Grief affects people in different ways. Some weep for weeks,
others go off their food and a few seek solace in the bottle.

When his wife died, Robert Hawker called for some cream for
consolation. For week after week he would eat nothing else –
gallons of the stuff disappeared down his throat at breakfast
time, lunch and supper.

The uncontrolled flow of calories only stopped when he was
so violently sick that he refused to touch it again.

A Rare Treat

The guests of Lord Eyre always fed on the same meat – a freshly
slaughtered ox that was hung up whole over the table. Guests
were expected to help themselves to it, and Eyre was very upset
if anyone refused.

The meals went on from lunchtime until well into the night
and the stench lingered around for days – not one window of
the castle would open.

Show me the Way to Go Home

Beauchamp Bagenal's dinner guests were often taken home after the feasts that he prepared for them. Not, however in one of the fine carriages that he kept, but lying inert on a handcart!

Bagenal refused to let anyone leave his groaning table until every last crumb had been devoured and every last drop drunk.

The genial host kept two pistols by his side. One to shoot the top off the wine barrel — the other to shoot any guests who attempted to leave the table while still sober.

Thirsty Work

An eighteenth century Welshman was in the habit of reading the Bible every morning for two hours; not because he was desperate to lead a better life, but because he took it into his head that if he drank as many gallons of ale in the evening as chapters he had read in the morning, his constitution would be able to cope with the excess of alcohol.

He must have been a quick reader, for towards the end of his life he was knocking back at least eight gallons (64 pints) a day.

It was one way of quenching his thirst for knowledge.

The Toast of the Town

Nothing should be allowed to interfere with an Englishman's breakfast — not even the fire that broke out in the London hotel where Osbert de Vere Beauclerk was taking his morning meal.

Osbert stoically ordered more tea while firemen rushed around him, trying to prevent the whole building being toasted.

CREATORS OF HAVOC

**Incredible inventors, batty builders
and abnormal artists.**

Alternative Deaths

James Puckle believed that the Turk deserved to die more painfully than his Christian brothers.

Accordingly, the machine gun that he invented in 1722 had two types of bullets — round ones for those who had had the benefit of baptism and square ones, which were much more painful, to be used when firing at Turkish enemies.

Belt Up

Mr C. B. Harness's Electropathic Belt was one of the oddest inventions of all time. It was said to 'improve the figure and prevent chills, as well as renew exhausted nerve form.'

It was a battery-operated appliance strapped around the user's midriff that delivered electric shocks at regular intervals.

It didn't work, of course, but Mr Harness made a great deal of money out of his crazy corset.

Running Water in Every Room

When Edgar Kaufmann asked architect Frank Lloyd Wright to make the most of the picturesque site he had chosen for his house, he little suspected that Wright would plan to build OVER the waterfall that cascaded through his green acre.

But that's just what the famous architect did. The water roars over the falls directly underneath the three-storey cantilevered building.

Perhaps he was trying to plumb the depths.

A Stitch in Mime

Better known for his creation of the phonograph, Thomas Edison also invented a sewing machine — powered by the human voice.

Sound waves were converted into power, driving the device, which *did* work.

Unfortunately, the machine's popularity was short-lived since the owners had to shout at a very loud pitch for hour after hour to make the contraption sew efficiently. This resulted in sore throats, lost voices and, eventually, lost orders.

Moving House

An American millionairess loved the house that she had bought, but hated the location.

She ordered that the foundations be dug up and the whole shooting match be moved to a new site — on rollers.

She and her husband had to move out, naturally, but their possessions stayed inside while their home was on the move; and they did pop in every night to change for dinner!

Sun Stroked

A Belgian aristocrat decided to move to Cairo to take advantage of the perpetual sunshine. He bought a site to build his house on and set about the task.

His residence was built atop a turntable that moved slowly round all day so that the Baron's favourite room always faced the sun.

Titfer T'at

In an age when it was considered *de rigeur* for gentlemen to wear hats Sir Francis Galton became obsessed with the idea that lack of ventilation was bad for the head and hair. His solution to the problem raised quite a few eyebrows.

His Universal Patent Ventilating Hat looked like an ordinary top hat until Sir Francis squeezed the rubber valve in his hand. A tube conducted the current of air from the valve to the hat, causing the crown to lift off.

Sir Francis was more than happy with his invention, and the startling effect it had on passers-by did little to dissuade him from wearing it all the time, indoors and out.

A Bloody Good Idea

£4,000 a year didn't go very far for Richard Pockrick. His hare-brained schemes lost him money at an alarming rate.

His substantial investment in a scheme to convert the Bishop of Tuam's palace outside Dublin was lost when His Grace refused to remove.

His scheme to convert the Irish peat bogs into vineyards was as fruitless as the vines that were planted.

He eventually became obsessed with the idea that blood transfusions could give the recipients eternal life. When it was pointed out that a world without death could pose many problems, especially for those who were waiting for inheritances, Pockrick had the answer ready.

An Act of Parliament was to be passed declaring that anyone who made it to the age of 999 was to be deemed legally dead. This would allow heirs to claim their estates and the clergy to claim burial fees for the legally 'dead', but in reality still alive-and-kicking 999 year-olds.

On a Different Wavelength

Three thousand citizens of Northgate in Seattle gathered in the local Shopping Precinct one day to watch the unveiling of the latest work by a local sculptor whose lunacy was legend.

At a given signal the cloth covering was removed to reveal an enormous statue of Abraham Lincoln. Its creator was delighted with the warm response of the assembled crowd.

He then pressed a button and the statue's arms began to move in an alarmingly lifelike way. Another switch operated the Presidential jaw and the lips began to move. A third switch operated the tapedeck inside Mr Lincoln's enormous head and the words of one of his famous speeches boomed across the town, amplified by two powerful speakers in the arms.

The appreciative gasps of astonishment soon turned to roars of laughter as the famous politician's words faded away and those of a dubious popular song echoed through Northgate.

Abraham's recreator had forgotten to check the waveband and a powerful local signal had interrupted the solemn and historic Declaration of Independence.

Who Was Odder?

A woman wanted a 'nice statue' to mark the spot where her dear-departed dog was buried. A cupid, she suggested to the sculptor she commissioned, or an angelic child holding a puppy.

The artist assured her that he would think of something appropriate – and he did. A seven-foot-high glass fibre lamp post.

'I think the dog would have appreciated it,' he said in court when suing the woman for refusing to pay his fee. 'A lamp post is a dog's best friend.'

RIP

RUFUS

The Welbeck Wonder

William Cavendish Bentinck-Scott enjoyed being in the pink. All the rooms that he added to his ancestral home, Welbeck Abbey, were painted that colour.

He was a compulsive builder. The new apartments all opened on to a stunning Rose Corridor, a long, glass-roofed conservatory. One of the many libraries that he built could hold twelve billiard tables, and 2,000 people could dance the night away in the ballroom, which, like the rest of the place, was centrally heated and lit by thousands of gas jets. To reach the ballroom a lift capable of holding twenty people was installed, carrying them down into the bowels of the Earth.

Bentinck-Scott's creations were all built underground. So was the railway that carried the food 150 yards from the kitchen to the dining room, and the roadway that could carry carriages two-abreast to Worksop, over a mile away.

But the whole extravagant subterranean folly never echoed with the tinkling giggles of beautiful women or the raucous laughter of port-filled gentlemen swapping ribald stories among themselves, for Bentinck-Scott was also a recluse and no one was ever invited to Welbeck to enjoy its sumptuous splendour.

See Through

When William Roentgen discovered X-rays in 1895, one enterprising underwear manufacturer, reading that some journalists were convinced that the primary users of the new discovery would be Peeping Toms, marketed and sold several pairs of X-ray-proof knickers.

It wasn't long, however, before his customers saw through his invention and he was forced into liquidation.

A Modest Little Dwelling

When Mrs Sarah Winchester moved into her house in San Jose, California it was an ordinary type dwelling. She decided to enlarge it, and for the next 38 years kept scores of carpenters, plumbers and masons busy almost all of the time.

Some of the rooms she had built were as sumptuous as a royal throne room, decorated with gold and silver chandeliers, stained-glass windows, inlaid floors and satin-covered walls. Other rooms were built simply, enabling Mrs Winchester to hear the reassuring sound of men at work.

The house had rooms a few inches square, stairways that led nowhere and passages that ended at blank walls. When she died in 1922, the house had eight storeys, three lifts, 48 fireplaces, nine kitchens and miles of secret passageways and hallways. It sprawled over six acres and had 160 rooms.

The cost of all this? $5,000,000.

L'Arc d'Elephant

Late eighteenth-century French people had a taste for grandiose architecture, and one man who was always ready to pander to their taste was architect Charles Ribart.

One of his schemes was unfortunately turned down by the French government who were planning to build on the spot where the Arc de Triomphe now stands.

Ribart designed a splendid three-storey building with a ballroom, entered into by way of a spiral staircase. The structure was to be air-conditioned and have furniture that folded into the wall. The whole building was shaped like an elephant and the drainage system was incorporated into its trunk.

A Screwy Idea

In the 1920s, when dimples were fashionable, a patent was filed in the US Patent Office for a machine designed to produce artificial ones. Those in search of dimpled beauty were exhorted to press bullet-shaped screws into their chins and cheeks to produce the desired clefts.

In the same year, a patent was lodged for a tongue shield to stop the taste of unpleasant medicines. The only drawback was that once the device was fitted, it was impossible for the wearer to swallow!

A Fertile Imagination

Mr Arthur Pedrick, who describes himself as a 'One-Man-Think-Tank Basic Physics Research Laboratory', has patented several machines including a motor car that could be driven from the back seat!

But the grand-daddy of all his ideas was his scheme to irrigate the deserts of the world by bombarding them with a constant stream of snowballs despatched from the Polar Regions by a network of giant wind-powered peashooters.

(True – honestly!)

The Art of Eccentricity

Artists are, generally speaking, an eccentric bunch but the work of Dennis Oppenheim is odd by any standards. One 'work' of his is a photograph called *Reading Position for a Second Degree Burn*. To produce it, Oppenheim lay in the scorching sun with an open book placed facedown on his chest. The photograph showed the artist's severely burned body with a virgin white rectangle where the book had been.

Oppenheim made a movie of his own face as he stood in the middle of a small circle of people throwing stones at him.

Oppenheim's work was almost outdone by a piece exhibited by sculptor Carl Andre. It consisted of five hundred pounds of cheese anointed with ten gallons of ketchup. The cheese was ten inches thick. The exhibition opened on 19 January, 1973 and closed the next day.

The Artist's Palate

Chinese artist Huang Erh-nan paints breathtakingly beautiful pictures. They are delicately executed and the soft colours glow like candlelight.

Huang's technique is peculiar to say the least. When he gets down to work he takes a mouthful of black ink, leans over his table and licks the paper with his tongue.

The Sudbury Daedalus

Jack Gainsborough liked cuckoos, so much so that he made a mechanical one that sang all year round. This he perched in an apple tree in his garden.

Jack was also fond of apple dumplings – so he hung the tree with dozens of them and lay happily in its shade, the bird singing in his ear, his favourite food an arm's length away.

His real ambition was to take to the air, but the pair of copper wings that he built didn't work, no matter how hard he flapped them, standing on a branch of the dumpling tree with the appropriate bird song giving him encouragement: 'Cuckoo, Cuckoo.'

A Waspish Invention

Sir David Sitwell, father of Osbert, Sacheverell and Edith, was so annoyed by a plague of wasps which threatened to drive him from his Derbyshire home, that he designed and had made a tiny pistol to shoot them.

Otherwise Engaged

A crackpot inventor was always annoyed when he climbed the stairs to the lavatory, only to find it occupied. So, in order to avoid unnecessary journeys, he wired it for sound.

He hung a microphone in the water closet and one by the towel rail. Speakers were scattered around the house. No matter where he was he knew if the facilities were being used!

A Suicidal Folly

Plans to build a 100-foot-high folly on an Oxfordshire estate had so enraged local residents that they went to court to prevent it, but the cranky owner won the day and the outrageous building was duly completed.

The building was formally dedicated to complete uselessness, this being confirmed by the inscription above the door:

'Members of the public committing suicide from this tower do so at their own risk.'

Shocking Treatment

A French doctor's cure for constipation was so outlandish that it is surprising that he found a willing human guinea pig. But one poor woman was so plagued by her lavatorial inability that she was persuaded to submit herself to the curious cure.

One end of a piece of wire was attached to the patient's navel and the other was inserted into the obstinate orifice. A short surge of electricity had very positive results within two minutes.

Not surprising!

MAD MENAGERIE

**Characters whose oddity involves
animals.**

A Lavish End

The deceased lay in state for several days in his silk-sheeted bed. His diamond ring shone in the light of the silver candelabra and an ornate, gold crown glittered on his head.

After all the tributes had been made, he was lowered into the ground in a coffin covered with 1,000 carnations.

Not being of a religious nature, no hymns were sung or prayers said – instead poems by Keats and Shelley were recited.

The recipient of all this royal adulation and honour? A beloved pet *parrot* of a cranky US millionaire!

A Bird in the Hand

One hermit spent so long in prayer during Lent that a blackbird nested in his cowl.

The good man did not move until the bird had hatched her eggs several weeks later and the fledglings had left the nest.

By rights they should have been hooded crows.

Enormous Sentimental Value

A South American man was distraught when his pet cat was stolen from his Rio de Janeiro house. The police recovered it a few days later, which was hardly surprising. The cat-thief had found it very difficult to conceal a full-grown lion!

Feline and owner were happily reunited. The big cat was of great sentimental value to the man. It had eaten his best friend during a hunting expedition!

A Real Swined Instrument

Abbé Debaigne, music master at the court of Louis XI of France, devised one of the oddest musical instruments ever. He picked twelve pigs, each with a different pitched squeal, and arranged them in scale order.

A keyboard came next, connecting the appropriate keys by sharp-pointed wires to the backs of the poor swine. When the keys were depressed, the wires prickled the appropriate pigs, who squealed loudly, producing the desired tune.

Lucky Dogs

Irish landowner Edward Eyre set off for the races one day in his fine carriage. He was dressed as usual in fine silks and perfectly chosen accessories.

Accompanying him were Dapper and Kitsey, their heavy brocade skirts carefully arranged so that they would not crease, jewels sparkling round their elegant necks.

The family's pedigree was impeccable. Edward could trace his ancestry back to one of the greatest families in Ireland. Dapper and Kitsey were two of the most perfectly bred labrador bitches in the land.

A Right Mug

A Philadelphia man had an odd way of protecting himself against muggers. He carried in his bag a ten-foot long python!

The unfortunate reptile met a sad end when it bit a policeman who promptly clubbed it to death.

Society's Court Jester

Ward McAllister spread the news that the guest of honour at his next party was a fabulously wealthy Indian.

Vanderbilts, Astors, Morgans and all the best families fought for invitations to the glittering reception that was to launch the potentate amongst them.

His arrival caused gasps of astonishment – for the mighty mogul turned out to be an enormous, long tusked elephant! It was another of McAllister's renowned practical jokes.

Canine Justice

A certain Irish landowner was very fond of his red setter, Gusty, but irritated by its habit of straying.

Every time it was brought back, the dog was severely reprimanded for keeping low company and put into solitary confinement for three days on bread and water.

After this had happened several times, the dotty dog lover told his pet that the next time he strayed he would be hanged, waving a piece of rope before the rheumy eyes of his friend, to emphasise the point.

The dog wandered off again and was duly recaptured. Being a fair man, the landowner decided to give him a fair trial. His foreman was appointed Counsel for the Defence, and the gardener Counsel for the Prosecution: the man himself sat in justice.

Two witnesses gave evidence of how Gusty had been found and resisted arrest. The jury deliberated for a few minutes before pronouncing the dog in the dock guilty.

The death sentence was pronounced, but happily no one would carry out the execution and master and setter were reunited.

I'll Drink to That

Ned Green hated drinking alone, but he was addicted to the bottle. As he sank into alcoholism it became more and more difficult to find a boozing companion.

His solution to the problem was novel to say the least! He bought himself a pet seal, which seemed to thrive on the bottle of twelve-year-old malt that Ned poured into its drinking bowl every day!

Like Long John Silver

Strollers in London's Regent's Park often stopped in their tracks at the sight of a famous actor, clad in leather, roaring round the Inner Circle on his powerful motorbike — his pet parrot on his shoulder.

The poor bird needed fresh air, but the chauffeur had refused to take it out in the Rolls after it had bitten his ear once too often.

Canine Stitches

The dog trotted round and round a moveable disc which was connected to a set of wheels that operated — a sewing machine.

Unfortunately the nutty professor who invented the contraption did not make his longed-for fortune out of it — Victorian animal lovers had it banned shortly after it was first marketed!

The Bite was Worse than the Bark

Guests at Walton Hall in Yorkshire had a great deal to contend with. There were toads in the bathroom, albino hedgehogs in the kitchen, wildlife wandered all over the stately pile.

But the worst thing was being constantly snapped at, growled at and bitten by the owner who spent most of his time on all-fours pretending to be a dog!

'Nice Horses'

Londoners were used to many strange sights, but the carriage and four that clip-clopped along Piccadilly stopped the fashionable men and women shopping there dead in their tracks.

Heads turned as the equipage rounded the Circus and turned down the Haymarket, round Trafalgar Square, under Admiralty Arch, up the Mall and into the forecourt of Buckingham Palace.

Queen Alexandra peered at the beasts pulling the carriage and put her hand out to stroke the 'nice horses'.

Lord Rothschild alighted from the carriage and warned Her Majesty, who was a little short-sighted, that the 'horses' were, in fact, wild zebras, quite liable to snap off her regal fingers.

Excess Passengers

History does not record the name of the unfortunate passenger with whom naturalist Francis Buckland once shared a carriage to London.

The man nodded off to sleep a few minutes after Buckland had dropped off. When the zoologist wakened he was horrified to see the giant red slugs he had been carrying crawling across the sleeping passenger's bald head, preparing to mate with each other.

Discretion is the better part of valour, and Buckland, who was unafraid of any wild beast, quickly left while the slumbering man snoozed on, unaware of the slugging match going on above.

A Non-Ewe Bequest

John Leeming wrote a biography of his best friend.
 One of the Family was all about Clwyd, his pet ram, who followed Leeming like a lemming whenever he went out, and inherited £30,000 when his master died.

Brace Yourself

Charles Waterton, adventurer and explorer extraordinary, was quite set on capturing the notoriously dangerous boa constrictor alive.
 His bearers tried to talk him out of it, but, on encountering the fearsome reptile, Waterton rushed up to it, grabbed it by the head and sat astride it, before binding up its venomous mouth — with his braces!
 He was also known to ride alligators!

Neigh, my Lord

The nineteenth century Irish Earl, Lord Waterford, became widely known for his zany pranks and quixotic behaviour.

After one rapscallion escapade the noble earl was brought before a judge on a charge of reckless driving.

Only one witness could testify to his innocence (or guilt), declared Waterford, and called his thoroughbred carriage horse into the witness box.

The case was dismissed and the unabashed earl rode triumphant from the court room.

Well Collared

Lord Berners could well afford to indulge his crazy caprices, so no one who knew him was in the least surprised when he ordered new collars for his numerous dogs.

Each one was studded with diamonds, emeralds and rubies, causing one friend to remark that Berners had created the original rich bitch.

Youthfully Eccentric

Eccentricity is usually associated with old age – but this is not always the case.

Take, for example, one young Yorkshire lad who was expelled from his boarding school for teaching his pet to jump hurdles when he should have been studying.

That may seem a bit drastic; after all, what schoolboy has not been caught in some similar escapade or prank?

The headmaster, however, felt himself entirely justified – *pigs* should, in his opinion, be kept for farrow or bacon, not harnessed and ridden over fences!

Goodnight Brayers

What more could a man ask for? The dinner had been superb. The food had been eaten with all the relish with which a lapsed dieter falls on a box of chocolate mints. Glass after glass of fine wine had ensured that the conversation was as sparkling as the best champagne.

What more could a man want? The host had thought of that, too. Or so one of the guests thought as he climbed into his bed and found it already occupied.

A few seconds later he was running down the oak-panelled corridors of Waterford House, scared out of his befuddled mind by the noisy response of his nightgowned companion to his first amorous advances.

His host, Lord Waterford, a renowned practical joker, had put a fully-grown donkey into the unfortunate man's bed!

An Entrancing Entrance

Jack Mytton's guests chatted amongst themselves as they waited for their host. Conversation came to a complete halt as frightening growls were heard in the passage-way outside.

A wild dog? A wolf even?

The mystery was soon solved when the doors crashed open and the happy host made his spectacular entrance, roaring with laughter and sitting astride a fully-grown brown bear.

His tears of mirth turned into tears of pain when he fell off and the frightened beast bit him in the leg. Mr Mytton had no choice but to grin and bear it.

Tales from the Registrar

The Chief Registrar at Caxton Hall, the now defunct Registrar's Office in London, was used to odd ideas from his clients, but even he was taken aback by the ridiculous request of one would-be bride who demanded that her two pampered poodles act as witnesses to the ceremony.

A Dazzling Orifice

As he trundled along on the back of his brightly-decorated elephant, one fabulously wealthy Maharaja must have felt threatened by the sight of the anal orifice of the beast in front of him in the procession, for when he returned to his palace he summoned his goldsmith and ordered him to make an emerald-studded 'plug' to be inserted in the offending opening whenever the regal procession left home.

The Ebullient Huntsman

Several spectators who had gathered in the market square to watch the hunt gather edged as far away as possible from the plump, jolly-looking farmer, sitting astride his mount.

His breeches were as white as his fellow huntsmen. His boots were as highly polished and his coat as scarlet as theirs – and the *bull* he was sitting on didn't seem to mind the foxhounds snapping round its bovine hooves!

A Little Monkey Business

Guests at Lord Rothschild's Buckinghamshire house were puzzled when they went in to dinner. They found themselves seated with an empty chair between each of them. Perhaps, they thought, there were more guests to arrive. There were.

Just before the first course was served, the doors swung open and the missing invitees walked in to their places. The males were properly dressed in white tie and tails, and their partners in silk frocks and sparkling jewels. The only strange thing about his lordship's latecomers was – that they were monkeys!

Dazzling Doves

One colourful crackpot thought the doves that fluttered around his Oxfordshire estate were unspeakably dull, so he ordered his gamekeeper to catch them all and dye each one a different colour. Soon the skies were filled with the rainbow-hued birds, cooing softly as they flew from dovecote to trees.

Visitors thought the whole idea quite coo-coo, too.

Lucky Cow

The Maharaja of Baroda liked all his women to be decked out in jewels and could well afford to pamper them all.

One rather large female was given ten gold chains to hang from her ears, each worth £25,000.

The Maharaja loved being carried around on her back — she was a full-grown cow elephant.

THE ARISTOCRANKS

**Peculiar people from the ranks of
the peerage.**

Feeling Sweepy

Catherine, Duchess of Queensberry, was not a great one for subtlety, as three distinguished politicians found out to their embarrassment.

The Duchess was furious when the trio withdrew from a large party into a small room in her London house one night. There would be no doors barred in her house, the Duchess decided, and instructed a startled footman to unscrew the offending portal. The shame-faced parliamentarians rejoined the other guests, but took their leave at the first opportunity.

Had they not left so promptly, the redoubtable lady would doubtless have used her favourite, equally unsubtle way of getting rid of guests who outstayed their welcome. She simply picked up a broom and began to sweep the floor, thus giving her friends the brush off.

She Lasted a Day

The large, aristocratic lady working in a top-people's store whose customers are said to enter a different world, had fallen on hard times and had been forced to take a job demonstrating a houshold cleaner called Shift.

At lunchtime on her first day her lawyers called to tell her about an unexpected windfall.

A woman of honour, she felt that she could not simply walk out, so she set about getting herself fired – spectacularly.

She continued to demonstrate the product, but dropped the 'f' from its name, as she exhorted people to buy it . . . .

This expedient was entirely satisfactory – she received her cards the very same day.

Up to his Neck in It

When Lord Rokeby went to Aix la Chapelle in the late 1750s to take the waters he little suspected just how much the *eau* was going to change his *vie*.

Almost from the first moment that he submerged himself in the health-giving water he decided that from then on he was going to spend as much time as possible up to his neck in it.

When he returned to England he built a beach hut at Hythe and walked the three miles from his home, there and back, every day — fair weather or foul. He did not just *like* his amphibious life, he gloried in it, and preached its virtues to anyone who would listen.

If he felt peckish during his sub-aqua stints he nibbled the knuckle of veal that he always kept close to hand, bobbing around in the waves.

The old aristocrat spent so much time pretending to be a fish that he sometimes passed out in the water. When he did so flounder, his servant, whose sole duty was to keep a sharp eye on his master from his seat on the bleak beach, waded in to the rescue. He became a dab hand at fishing Rokeby out of the brine.

A Uniformed Nobleman

At first, the friends of Harry Barry were surprised when he joined them for dinner dressed as a liveried footman, but they soon became used to his odd dress. He had good reason for it.

His debts were so enormous that creditors and bailiffs were always on his tail. If ever any of them managed to find out where he was, employing his simple disguise, he left his chair and joined the servants waiting table in the dining room.

The Lucky Butler

The 3rd Marquis of Hertford's dying words summed up his extraordinary outlook on life. 'They tell me that my place in Wales is very fine,' he gasped. 'I have never seen it. A dinner for twelve is served there every day . . . the butler eats it.'

The marquis had never met the grateful servant, either.

Sex Discrimination

The 9th Earl of Orford endeared himself to many ladies of his acquaintance so strongly that the upper classes were liberally sprinkled with the fruits of his illicit liaisons.

The Earl was more than willing to care for his illegitimate offspring, on one condition – that they all, regardless of whether they were male or female, bore the same name, Horace Walpole (4th Earl of Orford and famous 18th century 'Gothic' novelist).

The Roof of Friendship Fund

Friends of Lady Sackville received a letter from her one day, asking them to donate the price of a tile which was to be used to build a roof, to 'form an inspirational symbol of friendship'.

Several of the persuasive lady's friends were charmed by the idea and sent off their cheques. (William Nicholson actually sent a tile!)

What the Baroness had failed to mention in her note was that the roof in question was her own, which was in sorry need of repair.

The Weight of the Monarchy

Many people felt sorry for the Queen when she had to bear the heavy weight of St Edward's Crown for a long part of her Coronation.

One elderly aristocrat was moved to such a depth of sympathy that, in order to share his sovereign's plight, he sat and watched the entire service on television, fully robed and with a vast copy of Debrett's Peerage on his head.

Ne'er a Drop

'I have never,' the old French aristocrat said to a newspaper reporter towards the end of the last century, 'allowed water to pass my lips since I was eighteen. Wine, and only wine. That's the secret of my longevity.'

The journalist smiled and said, 'But surely M. le Vicomte, when you brush your teeth . . .'

'For that,' the old man replied, 'I recommend a very light Sauterne!'

The Grand Duke's Nightingale

In pre-Revolutionary Russia, many of the more important landowners owned their own opera houses where they presented lavish entertainments to impress their friends.

One such aristocrat asked the great bass singer Feodor Chaliapin to come to his palace to discuss a performance. Chaliapin was immediately aware of the beautiful song of a nightingale coming from the Grand Duke's garden, as soon as he entered the salon.

All the way through their discussions, the bird sang magnificently. Chaliapin was puzzled, for it was winter and nightingales should have migrated from Russia. He remarked on the birdsong to the Duke who smiled and said that he could not be without his nightingale. Conversation closed.

When he was being shown out by the Duke's butler, the singer mentioned the nightingale to him. The butler took him into the garden and Chaliapin was stunned at the sight that awaited him. For there, perched on a tree, was a serf whistling in perfect imitation of the nightingale.

The Power of Wealth

La Comtesse de Noalles could well afford to buy anything that caught her fancy – including the daughter of a Spanish artist, whom she came across in Paris and took it into her head that she would like to adopt. That little purchase cost her two bags of gold.

La Comtesse had very strict ideas of how her adopted daughter was to be brought up. She was sent to school, of course – St Leonard's in Sussex.

Unfortunately the lake nearby looked as if it could be a breeding ground for germs. Would the school arrange to have it drained? The governors agreed.

There was only one cow in the herd of a nearby farmer that looked as if it would provide milk worthy of Maria. Would the school arrange that Maria had that, and only that? The Governors agreed.

The school uniform was quite unsuitable for her daughter. Would the governors mind if Maria wore a Greek tunic and sandals? Of course not.

La Comtesse also thought that the curriculum was not what she had in mind and arranged that special tutors instruct Maria in her own system of grammar and mathematics.

With such a dotty mother, it is surprising that Maria grew up to be a normal, well-adjusted girl.

But even after the old lady died, she still got her way as far as Maria was concerned. She left her all her money on condition that she only wore white in summer and never wore laced shoes.

Good Shot, Sir

The eighth Earl of Bridgwater was a celebrated English
eccentric of the eighteenth century. He liked nothing better
than shooting, but when his eyesight began to fail it was
difficult for him to make his way across the moors.

He got round this trifling difficulty by having his garden
stocked with partridges and pigeons: with clipped wings. There
were so many birds that all he had to do was hang out of his
window and fire in any direction, being reasonably sure that he
would hit some poor bird. Fowl behaviour, perhaps.

He also had an odd way of recording the passage of time. He never wore a pair of shoes for more than one day and when he had finished with them he had them arranged in rows so that he could see time passing. Was this perhaps the derivation of the phrase, 'time marches on'?

Untouched by Human Hand

The first Marquis of Abercorn was very conscious of his high station in life. So were his servants.

His household staff were under strict instructions never to hand anything to their noble master unless they had first dipped their fingers in rose water to remove the merest suggestion of an offensive smell.

His lordship also could not bear the thought that his bed had been made by anything so common as a housemaid's hands or his sheets tainted by a tweeny's touch. Before anyone was allowed to plump the pillows or smooth the bed linen, they had to put on white kid gloves especially provided by the fastidious marquis.

Too Much on his Plate

A wild-looking Irishman booked in to a Spanish hotel signing himself on the register 'Aldborough'. He asked that his meals be sent up to him in his room.

They were — every day for two months. But the plates were never returned.

The guest refused to let anyone into his room to tidy up.

After eight weeks there were dishes piled everywhere. Lettuce leaves littered the floor. Platefuls of paella were stacked on top of each other. The smell was overpowering.

Still, the bills were always paid on the nail every Friday.

When there was no room left in the room to move, the loony lodger asked to be moved into another and the whole greasy cycle repeated itself every eight weeks until the extraordinary earl died.

Perhaps he had too much on his plate to cope.

Thou Shalt Not Look

The Duke of Somerset loved to be seen – but only by his peers.
In order to avoid unworthy eyes falling on his magnificent
personage he built fine houses between London and his West
Country estates, thus avoiding the necessity of staying at
common inns.

As he progressed to the peace and safety of his manor house,
an outrider went ahead clearing the road of working people.

He refused to speak to his servants, preferring to
communicate with them by an elaborate sign language that he
devised. One can imagine the sign they made to him as soon as
his noble back was turned.

A Different Ball Game

Two lady golfers who were making up a four with an
extraordinary Irish earl and a friend one day were given great
cause for embarrassment.

As his clothes were obstructing his lordship's swing, off they
came and the naked nutcase got down to addressing the ball,
while the ladies studiously addressed each other in order to
preserve their decorum.

The Eyes Had It

The madcap Marquis of Waterford had a novel way of dealing
with the problem of boredom during a stay in London.
Indulging in a little indoor target practice, he simply shot the
eyes out of every ancestral portrait hanging on the walls!

Fair Exchange

Guests at a London hotel were familiar with the pet hedgehog that had the run of the lobby. One day it disappeared.

It turned up a few weeks later at an inn several miles outside the city, far too far to have travelled there under its own steam!

The mystery was soon solved when the landlord explained that he had been talked into swapping it for a *spongecake* by a large aristocratic lady.

She turned out to be Lady Mary Cork, renowned for her inability to keep her hands off anything she fancied — the prickly subject of her little weakness was the talk of the town for many years in the eighteenth century.

Self Help

A certain Polish countess refused to let surgeons operate on the tumour in her breast. Instead she packed her bags and set off on a trip round Europe. Her family assumed that she was off to bid farewell to friends and visit favourite places before she died.

They should have known the old lady better.

She returned to Poland after a few months – in perfect health.

Her puzzled family later found out that she had bought a scalpel here, some scissors there: surgical needles in one place and thread in another. When she arrived in Paris she took rooms and removed her breast on her own, with no assistant whatsoever.

She lived for a further 19 years.

THERE'S NOWT AS QUEER AS...

Great eccentrics — who defy description!

Premature Burial

Mrs Emma Smith decided to get away from it all for a while so she had herself buried in a coffin one day in 1968 and there she stayed until she was ready to come out — 101 days later.

Food and drink were piped down to her and she could communicate with family and friends above ground by means of a close-circuit television hook up.

She was not the first person to do this. More than 130 years before, an Indian Yogi did the same, only without the comforts that Mrs Smith arranged for herself. He had himself wrapped in bandages and put into a hole in the ground.

Forty days later his followers dug him out. He had been in a state of suspended animation for all that time and woke up shortly after being unburied.

A Rude Awakening

William Strachey's little penchant for rising at tea time and dining when most people were taking breakfast meant that he did not have a chance to go out into the society that he so longed for.

He decided to break his routine and bought a bed to help him in his struggle to give up his odd addiction.

No ordinary bed! It was connected to an alarm clock and each morning when the bell shattered the peace of the snoring sleeper, the bed tipped him out onto the floor.

Unfortunately, it worked with such a violent action that Poor Bill was thrown right into a bathful of cold water nearby.

With his nightshirt dripping from his unwanted swim, Strachey picked up his stick, smashed the clock, pulled the bed to pieces and decided to return to his old ways.

Fatal Bad Breath

When a 68-year-old Polish immigrant in New York began to make bulk purchases of salt and garlic in his local grocery store, they put him down as 'a bit weird'.

As the weeks went by, they got used to their eccentric customer, who later explained that he needed the herb and flavouring not for some tasty Polish delicacy but to ward off vampires. For, he declared, 'New York was plagued with those eerie creatures and he felt that you couldn't be too careful.'

When the police subsequently called at his room to investigate his reported disappearance, they discovered that the poor Pole had been overcome in the end. There he lay, surrounded by salt and garlic – in a sock around his neck, in a bag around his waist, in the washing-up bowl, on the window sill – aromatically dead.

Had Count Dracula struck again? Were the streets of New York City after sunset now to be plagued with a halitosis-ridden ghoul? No, the cause of death was rather more mundane. He had choked to death – on a clove of garlic.

Warm Relief

The hissing of steam stopped the flow of conversation at a smart New York party one night.

It wasn't a gas leak, or a leak in the central heating – it was the host taking a leak in the fire place.

Jimmy Gordon sought relief whenever the urge came upon him, no matter where he was.

At least he had the manners to turn his back on society. Little wonder that society eventually turned its back on Jimmy and he was jailed as a public nuisance.

The Heston Hermit

The good folk of Heston tried to discourage local weirdo Johnnie Ives and move him on, but there was nothing that they could do. Ives had paid for the allotment and there was nothing in the lease to prevent him digging a huge hole, fitting a glass roof over it and moving his few paltry possessions in.

He lived in his 'hermitage' for several years in the first decade of this century with his small bedstead, oil stove and pots and pans.

He had, the police said, paid the (under)ground rent!

What Lovely Flowers, Mummy

Vita Sackville-West was one of this century's most flamboyant characters. Her mother was equally outrageous, if less notorious.

Both were keen gardeners – each in their own way. Vita created a famous garden at Sissinghurst – her mother had a much more straightforward approach. She liked artificial flowers.

Her garden was a riot of tin delphiniums ('Always in bloom and never troubled by slugs'), porcelain roses ('They look so clean after the rain'), velvet tulips ('The frost doesn't bother them at all') and satin geraniums ('Don't have to bother about bringing them in in winter').

Once, when Vita was coming for lunch and the garden was looking especially drab, she sent a friend out with money to buy more velvet, paper, silk and satin blooms and by the time her daughter arrived, the garden was restored to its usual riot of crazy colour.

He's the S-Winner

Sergei Kelnikov holds the world record! 23 minutes 14 seconds.
  That's how long he kissed a pig for. (I don't know what the
prize for his endeavour was, but I hope he brought back the
bacon.)

A Stall Story

Bewildered music lovers could hardly believe their eyes.
Celebrated pianist-composer Percy Grainger left the piano
during a break in the soloist's part, jumped off the stage and
began to run round the auditorium.

Up the centre aisle he ran, round the back of the stalls, down
the side, along the front, up the aisle again, round the other
side, his tailed coat flying behind him, his head held stiffly
upright by the white bow tie and peaked collar.

The concert hall echoed to the gasps of astonishment of the
audience and the 'clump, clump' of the ex-Army surplus boots
that completed his outfit.

Then, having completed his circuit, he jumped back on stage,
took his seat by the piano and made his entry — right on cue.

The Last Straw

The Warner family were used to the odd behaviour of their
butler, but even they found his performance at dinner one night
a little too much.

As well as being a man with his own peculiar ideas of how
things should be done, he was also a little too fond of the
decanter. On this particular evening, after spilling a liberal
amount of hollandaise sauce over the hostess's dress, he was
given a note by the sauce-smothered woman. 'You're drunk,' it
read. 'Leave the room at once.'

The butler, without looking at the note, placed it on a silver
salver and, supposing it was meant for the guest of honour,
lurched up the table and presented the piece of paper to — Sir
Winston Churchill.

Feet of China Clay

When the honourable member for King's Lynn decided to do something, he acted immediately.

He arrived home from the House one day and announced to his startled daughter that he was bored with politics and had decided to go and live in China.

'When?' she asked.

'Thursday,' he replied.

Within three days the servants had been paid off, the furniture stored and the luggage packed.

At eleven o'clock on the appointed day, the bored parliamentarian came out of doors, where his daughter waited for him. A few raindrops fell on his head.

'My dear child, it's raining. We won't go,' he cried. Then he hailed a hackney and drove off to the House.

They never did go. After that the farthest East he ever went was to his Norfolk constituency.

Hot Foot

Time and again neighbours had to restrain John Lewis from dashing into his burning bungalow in Saint Andrews.

Poor John was forced to stand and watch as the flames destroyed his brand-new bicycle, melted down his collection of cameras and binoculars, and the £4,000 in banknotes that he had tucked away went up in smoke.

It wasn't the fact that he was now without wheels that upset him so much, nor even that he could no longer be snap happy or long-sighted: the money was only money, after all; but his best pair of shoes had gone too!

An Obvious Answer

How do you keep your clothes dry when it is raining?

The answer was quite obvious to Frank Galton – take 'em off and sit on them until the storm is over.

That's what he used to do throughout his three score and more years – and he never even had a cold in the head.

The Grass is Greener . . .

Lord Kitchener astonished guests at a party in Calcutta when he showed them the bright green lawn. They knew that it hadn't been there a few days before and were mystified by its sudden miraculous appearance.

Kitchener refused to let them even approach the lawn. Had they done so, they would have discovered the secret known only to himself and the army of coolies who had slaved for 24 hours – the 'grass' was, in fact, mustard and cress.

Wherever his guests had *dejeuner*, it was certainly not *sur l'herbe*.

Up the Pole

Simeon Styllites lived for thirty years on top of a column, sixty feet high. There he prayed for hour after hour, day after day.

Sometimes he stood erect with his arms outstretched in the form of a cross, but more usually he lay on his back and brought his head forwards to meet his knees, reciting his rosary while he performed 1,244 sit-ups!

An Attractive Idea

Frank Galton had a theory that two people attracted to each other would lean together if seated side by side. If they sat bolt upright, there was no attraction whatsoever.

To prove his theory, he had pressure drums fitted to the chairs around his dining table and when his guests had gone home he examined the imprints they had left.

Skiing Dune Hill

Hadji Abderrahmane loves to ski.

No matter that he lives in Salah in Southern Algeria where snow is as scarce as a nun in a nightclub.

Hadji skis down the sand dunes, his voluminous Arab robes flowing out behind him, dark glasses protecting his eyes from glow-glare.

He Did Believe What He Said

A retired major firmly believed that all those over sixty 'whose continued existence does not benefit the community' should be put down.

True to his conviction, the outrageous officer covered himself with a Union Jack and shot himself on Margate promenade the day after his sixtieth birthday.

In the Glass House

John Berwick was understandably annoyed when he came home one night and found that the GPO had demolished his home. He had spent what little he could afford to make it comfortable. A few pot plants had added a splash of colour.

True, it was a bit cramped and he was, strictly speaking, a squatter, but John felt that the Post Office could have forewarned him what they planned to do.

The authorities refused to listen to John's complaint. His dwelling was their property – as are all the other *phone boxes* in the United Kingdom.

A Long Week's Work

A London woman took a temporary job in an Oxford Street store for the pre-Christmas rush. After her week was up she was asked if she would come back for the sales . . . her few months stretched on and on.

Every Monday she decided to hand in her notice the following Friday, but when the day came she reconsidered and thought that she would give it just one more week.

As she said at her farewell party – fourteen years later – 'I hate this place and the only way I could get through the week was knowing that I was resigning the next Friday.'

The Anti-Evaporation Brigade

Pittsburg city fathers had a zany idea to prevent fog in the 1920s. They poured thousands of gallons of oil into the nearby Ohio river, believing that this would prevent moisture forming in the air above the city.

The fog continued to roll in – surprise, surprise – but the Pittsburg powers-that-be had certainly created a more immediate problem – pollution on a colossal scale!

Violent Music

Colonel Borberry played the piano in a unique way – he shot at the notes with a Winchester repeater.

His fine way with a Steinway earned him a grand income in Edwardian music halls.

The Charge of the Farm Brigade

James Black's farm-hands were used to his outlandish ideas for improving their education, but they were puzzled when he ordered them to dig trenches, and build ramparts and battlements on his Staffordshire estate.

Was he expecting a visit from the bailiffs? Could he be planning to declare his land independent? Nothing would surprise them.

Their worst fears were confirmed when, a few days later, a motley band of local workers wearing motheaten military uniforms arrived at the farm.

The farmworkers were ordered to defend the fortifications and the locals were ordered to attack. Black took up position in an old oak tree and took potshots as battle commenced.

This rumbustious reenactment of the Battle of Sebastapol was Black's potty endeavour to bring history alive for his men. Secretly, however, they would much rather have been working the fields than fielding against the locals.

The Naked Truth

Warmly-clad duck hunters dropped their guns as well as their jaws whenever hair-brained Jack Mytton passed by on his way to the shoot.

He saw nothing wrong in braving the elements in his birthday suit. Stark naked, he pursued his prey across the frozen Shropshire countryside.

He warmed himself when he got home – eight bottles of port and brandy saw to that, the best type of central heating.

Just a Little Extra

The superintendent of an English gasworks thought he knew just how to ensure that the pressure in the gas-holder was sufficient to provide for the extra demand every Sunday lunchtime.

He climbed up to the top with a deckchair and the Sunday newspapers and spent the morning there, quite convinced that his weight added that little extra pressure to cook the local householders' roasts to perfection.

An Armless Hobby

Sky diving is only for the most daring amongst us. One team in America are more daring than most.

All eight of them have had a limb amputated but this does not stop them jumping out of 'planes at 10,000 feet and free falling until their 'chutes open.

Their name? *Pieces of Eight.*

Striking the Right Chord

Someone once said that *Parsifal* is the sort of opera that starts at six o'clock, and when you look at your watch three hours later find that it's only ten past.

The audience who witnessed the one and only performance of Riley's *Concert in C* agreed *en masse* with that sentiment. Every one of them, and several members of the orchestra, left before the last note had been struck.

The last note was exactly the same as the first . . . and the second . . . and the third . . . the same note was struck over and over again during the entire twenty minutes of the crazy concerto.

No one, had they stayed, would have realized that the orchestra as well as the audience was getting gradually smaller and smaller – the composer had specified that his repetitive rendition be performed entirely in the dark.

Stoned Out of His Mind

People stopped and stared whenever Simon Ellerton walked home. His clothes were quite ordinary and he was no freak, but the two large stones perched on top of his head caused much mirth among his neighbours.

The stones, Simon explained, would come in useful for building his cottage, just outside Durham.

The humble abode was years in construction but was eventually completed. By this time, however, Simon had become so used to his role of human hod that forever afterwards he considered himself improperly dressed unless his hat was held in place by two bricks.

The Two Cat Flaps

The man who visited the Professor of Oriental Languages in Dublin one day asked him why he had two holes at the bottom of his door.

They were, explained the Don, to allow his two cats to come and go as they pleased.

'Would one not do?' asked the puzzled visitor.

The academic looked at him scornfully. 'How could the big cat get in the little hole?'

'He wouldn't have to,' came the reply. 'But the little one could go through the big hole.'

'I never thought of that,' said the Professor.

It was the same great intellect who once translated *Gallia est omnis divisa in partes tres* as 'all Gaul is quartered into three equal halves.'

Hare Today, Gone Tomorrow

Hares were one Marylebone man's passion in life. The fact that he lived in the centre of London did not stop him attempting to ensure that lively leverets were always around.

Once a week he went into the country and trapped as many as he could, brought them back alive and released them in the busy streets among the trundling carriage wheels and omnibuses. Many an Edwardian worthy was startled out of his buttoned-up boots by the bobbing backside of a fleeing hare desperately trying to escape the busy traffic.

The hare-brained perpetrator of such bucolic battiness was finally bound over for a year when caught red-handed by the law in the act of producing a hare from his bag outside Marylebone Station.

Encore, Encore

It would be unkind to say that Florence Foster Jenkins had the voice of a frog. Unkind, that is, to the frog.

Despite her total lack of musical talent and her inability to sing in key, Florence toured the United States, packing 'em in wherever she went.

For her sell-out farewell recital at New York's Carnegie Hall, she began with *Ave Maria*, appearing on stage dressed as a nun. A pair of enormous wings were strapped to her shoulders. These shivered and shook with every mis-hit note that quivered from her tortured tonsils.

Blood Thirsty Royal

'Gun!'

A few seconds later a shot rang out. The peasant fell to the ground in the palace gardens below and Otto of Bavaria returned to his interrupted conversation – with the spirits in a cupboard in his bedroom.

A few seconds later the 'dead' peasant stood up, crept back into the palace and changed his rags for his liveried uniform.

Otto firmly believed that it was his duty to rid Bavaria of peasants and would have shot hundreds of them had his family not persuaded one of the servants to go through the same idiotic charade every day – and another to make sure that the King's gun was loaded with blanks.

Locked Away for Lock Picking

Albert Mannix's practised eye could pick out likely locks
hundreds of yards away, and, once selected, their owners had
no chance of retaining their possessions from the grasp of the
strangest thief ever recorded.

With amazing stealth, Albert would sneak up on his victim
and with one snip of his scissors the long tresses would be safely
in his pocket, often before the sheared girls realized what had
happened.

Albert was eventually caught in the act and sentenced to
three months hard labour.

A New Branch of Literature

Conversation came to a halt. Champagne glasses froze 'twixt hand and lip. The British Ambassador shrugged his shoulders and carried on talking to a fellow diplomat in the gardens of the British Embassy in Paris. The cause of this extraordinary interruption had been the sound of a sudden four-letter expletive rending the air. The sound of paper being ripped from a typewriter shattered the embarrassed silence. Then, as the clacking of keys resumed, the guests smiled and looked upwards.

There, sitting in the branches of a tree, was the Ambassador's notoriously extraordinary wife, typewriter perched on her knee, hard at work on her latest book. Leaves of paper fell to the ground and lay there until the diplomat's dotty wife finished her daily quota.

A few minutes later she climbed down and joined the guests, charming them with her witty conversation and opinions as unconventional as her way of working.

An Annual Swim

The good burghers of Copenhagen were astonished when a well-dressed Englishman jumped into the harbour there, swam to the other side and climbed out still wearing all his clothes, a top hat and carrying his umbrella.

He then hailed a carriage and drove back to his hotel.

Had the Danes talked to the townspeople of Windsor, Brighton and Killarny or the citizens of Seville or Lisbon or wherever the sartorial swimmer happened to be when he celebrated his birthday, they would have known that this was the peculiar way in which the younger son of a famous banking family marked the passing of another year.

Badly Brought Up

An Essex couple longed for a daughter, but when their only child was born they were disappointed. A lusty, bawling, bouncing baby boy was put into his mother's arms.

Not a pair to be deterred by such a trifling detail, the oddly determined parents took their baby home to the freshly-painted pink nursery, told all their friends that they had had their desired daughter and brought him up as a girl from that day onwards.

When Beatrice (for that is what he was christened) was twenty-four he fell foul of the law and it was only then that he found out that she wasn't a she but a he. He was astonished to be told that he was a male.

(This did happen in the early years of this century long before such subjects as sex education were on the school curriculum.)

Bathed in Diamonds

The fashionable French resort of Deauville was dazzled one year by a stunning girl who emerged from her bathing tent wearing a long white dress, sailor's hat, silk stockings and satin shoes covered with flashing diamonds and rubies. A huge diamond ring glittered on her right hand and her left arm was weighed down with bracelets.

She made her way to the water's edge and waded in, swam for a minute or two before emerging dripping wet, oblivious to the astonished gazes of the bewildered bathers.

A cheering crowd escorted her back to the changing tent. Half an hour later she came out in a simple gown and large picture hat, got into her cab and drove off.

She was never seen again — her appearance had been a mere flash in the sand.

DRIVEN TO DISTRACTION

Strange methods and motives of travel.

Ideas on His Own Station

When British Rail closed down the nearest station to one of our stately homes, its owner was incensed.

He continued to instruct his chauffeur to pick him up at the now-defunct depot whenever he travelled by train and simply pulled the communication cord when the locomotive passed through it.

As it ground to a halt, the aristocratic old man alighted, tipped the train driver a shilling and went to his car.

The Horsey Horseless Carriage

The first steam trams in San Francisco caused horses to panic in the streets. Horsedrawn vehicles were seen to career in all directions until Stan Mathewson came up with the answer.

He built a steam tram which could travel at eight miles an hour, fired by gas – *and shaped like a horse*.

It did the trick, surprisingly enough.

A Wet Walk

Crowds gathered around Manhattan's East River one day in 1899 to watch Professor Miller set off on his epic journey.

He solemnly strapped the four-feet-long, bark canoes to his feet and set out to walk from America to England.

He made it a few hundred yards before sinking – barking up the wrong sea.

He Should Be Locked Up

Jaromir Wagner wants to cross the Atlantic – in a cage. His plan is to persuade some ship's captain to tow his barrel-buoyed stainless steel box behind his ship, from Rotterdam to New York.

So far he has had no takers – perhaps the merchant navy doubts its pulling power.

A Little Healthy Exercise

After Georgy Bushuyev had a heart attack, his doctor told him to exercise a bit more than he had.

Georgy took the physician at his word and set out one day in 1973 from his house on the Baltic coast.

He arrived at the Pacific, 10,940 kilometres and 238 days later.

His Feet Never Touched the Ground

George Brummel, the famous Regency dandy, could not stand the idea of so much as a speck of dirt soiling the soles of his evening pumps and took his fastidiousness to extraordinary lengths.

His servants had orders to carry his sedan chair into his bedroom, pick him up and carry him to wherever he was bound, with instructions not to put him down until he was *inside* his host's house.

A Swanderful Car

The Indian race are used to the eccentricities of their former colonial masters, but even they were taken aback by the car that one cranky English civil servant imported from London.

It caused such a disturbance when it was driven through the streets of Calcutta that police had to advise its outraged owner to take it off the road.

Matthewson had not only imported the car, he had designed it himself, poring for hour after hour over his lonely drawing board until it was – perfect.

Perfection is in the eye of the beholder! The car was round and pointed with two wings wrapped around it, giving it the appearance of a ruptured refugee from *Swan Lake*. A long neck led from the body to an elegant head, complete with large yellow tusk.

When the driver wanted to attract attention to his mechanical masterpiece he pulled a lever in the dashboard which opened the tusk and shot spurts of hot steam at any unfortunate passer-by.

The horn was made of eight organ pipes, operated by the exhaust system, which also powered the musical keyboard underneath the dash.

A Miracle

People have swum the Channel, sailed across it in bathtubs, soap boxes and sinks. Only Walter Robinson has walked across it.

It took him eleven-and-a-half hours, before he strolled into Cap Gris Nez harbour where he removed the eight-feet-long water shoes on which he had achieved the extraordinary crossing.

Travelling Alone

It was odd that one gregarious composer who delighted in the company of his many friends loathed travelling in company. He went to extreme lengths to ensure that he got a compartment all to himself whenever he journeyed by train.

Fellow passengers scuttled past the heavily-bearded figure wearing enormous dark glasses, a large black topper and a voluminous black cloak, who beckoned them into his compartment.

Most ran past to another part of the train. The few who did venture into his company usually got off at the next station.

The mysterious passenger read his newspaper upside down, muttering to himself in a strange gobbledy-gook and every few minutes put a thermometer into his mouth to take his temperature.

If that did not get rid of them at the first attempt, the sharp knife that he played with did the trick at the next station!

A Swinging Journey

The constant shaking of trains upset the delicate constitution of a famous nineteenth century scientist whenever he was forced to travel.

To overcome this problem his manservant selected a comparatively empty compartment and slung a hammock between the luggage racks.

The eminent man spent the journey being rocked to and fro in his unorthodox bed to the considerable consternation of his fellow passengers. He was usually working on a manuscript, tied to him with thick cord around his waist, so no one dared interrupt him in order to complain.

Home James

Lord Curzon, like many of his class, had never dreamt of setting foot on an omnibus. A violent thunderstorm forced him to change his mind one day and he boarded the infradig vehicle in haste. As the 'bus swept past his front door he lept up, horrified to discover that public transport did not drop passengers off at their own thresholds!

From that day on, regardless of how short his journey on foot, his carriage followed him to prevent his being forced to suffer such indignity again.

QUIRKS OF PASSION

Odd behaviour in love and marriage.

Odd Society

A group of New York men have formed one of the most peculiar societies around.

The Ancient Order of Hen-pecked Husbands have dedicated themselves to standing up to their dominant wives.

Unfortunately, their Annual General Meeting had to be cancelled — none of the members was allowed to attend.

Laying Down the Lords

Queen Kahena, an eighteenth century Berber Queen, could perhaps teach today's feminists a lesson or two.

She kept a harem of 400 male concubines . . . obviously the nickname of our own late dear Queen Bess could never be applied to her.

Eyeless in Erin

The tenth-century Irish beauty whom history refers to simply as 'The Lady Derville' had no time for men. Not that she was in any way one of the girls who's one of the boys. Far from it. She had her sights set on a life of perfect purity.

Unfortunately, she was so beautiful that men came from all over Ireland to court her.

One outspoken suitor told the virginal Venus that her eyes were her most attractive feature — whereupon she pulled them out!

One could say that the eyes had it!

A Slight Case of Over-Reaction

'Be quiet, woman!' M. Regnier, French Royal Procurator, silenced his wife with these words after she had been prattling on about something of no interest to her husband.

Madame Regnier stormed out of the room into her chamber. There she stayed until her contrite husband went up to apologise to her a few hours later. His words were met with a stony silence. The hurt woman looked at him impassively and uttered not a word.

She maintained her silence from that day in 1842 until her death in 1872 – not one solitary word to one person.

A Consummating Interest

In the 1920s a certain Sir Thomas Medlicott asked the Duke of Sutherland if he could bring his bride to the ducal castle at Dunrobin to spend his honeymoon there. Sir Thomas was in his sixties: his fiancée in the first flush of youth.

After dinner the happy couple withdrew to their rooms and the Duke poured himself a snifter. An hour-and-a-half later the anxious bride burst into the library. 'Had the Duke seen her husband?' she asked. He had failed to arrive at the bedroom.

A search of the house was fruitless; as the now distraught girl became more and more hysterical the distant sound of an engine whistle was heard in the garden. There, to the bride's relief and the Duke's amusement, was the elderly bridegroom happily driving the famous Dunrobin Express – the double-track private railway built by the second duke during the Industrial Revolution.

We can only hope that Sir Thomas had not run out of steam by the time he eventually went to bed.

Quackers

The Registrar at Gretna Green has married many couples: starry-eyed youngsters too young to wed in their own countries; incurable romantics who think that a Gretna wedding is the foundation for lifelong happiness. She's married girls in jeans and men in leather jackets, but even she thought her eyes were playing tricks . . .

The groom came into the office wearing a dazzling white suit and the bride was carrying a leather suitcase. She asked if there was somewhere to change into her 'gown'.

A few moments later she emerged, not in a wonderful Emmanuel creation, but dressed as Donald Duck!

. . . And a Few Uninvited Guests

Percy Grainger, pianist, composer and conductor, was wildly eccentric.

During a tour of the United States, Grainger conducted a series of concerts at the famous Hollywood Bowl. So enthusiastic was he about the enormous stadium that he took it into his head that it would be a perfect venue for his forthcoming marriage.

Ever impulsive, Percy hurried his Scandinavian bride-to-be to the scene and, after the final note of the final concert, he laid down his baton, took his fiancée's arm and the happy couple were united in the eyes of God, the 128 piece orchestra and an astonished audience of 20,000 music-lovers.

Match that for an encore.

Out for the Count

The coffin was carried into the chapel. The priest nodded to the organist, who began to play, and the strains of *Here Comes the Bride* echoed round the church.

The bridegroom opened the coffin lid and took his place at the altar to await his lovely fiancée. He was dressed as Count Dracula. His four supporters were wearing green dayglo shrouds and the other guests were dressed as nuns, Vikings and cowboys.

The bride was in virginal white, a pearl choker around her neck: the only conventionally dressed person at the nuttiest nuptials over which the priest had presided.

Marry in Haste . . .

It had been a whirlwind courtship; the professor of Greek had fallen violently in love with the attractive heiress and married her within a few weeks of meeting her.

As soon as the service was over, the bride went home and the groom off to lunch with a friend, tarrying most of the afternoon over a good bottle of port, without once mentioning the events of the morning.

Lunch over, he went off to his club as usual, enjoyed a good chop and, having satisfied the inner man, went home to his lodgings, completely forgetting his eager bride until the next day when she came looking for him.

A Consummating Interest

Pop superstar Mick Jagger and his bride, Bianca, had retired to their hotel suite for their wedding night.

But their post-nuptial slumbers were rudely interrupted by a sudden rustling from outside the window.

The Rolling Stone rolled over and drew a gun from under his pillow, thinking that they were about to be attacked. A few seconds later *Who* drummer Keith Moon put his head through the curtains and said 'Good evening'.

He had climbed the eleven storeys to put the 'Moon' in honeymoon and bring his personal good wishes to the understandably furious couple.

A Statuesque Affair

Henry Jennings fell in love and installed his *inamorata* in his London house. The besotted man was never happier than when dining with his beloved – he at one end of the long, polished table, the object of his desires at the other, being waited on by the two liveried servants appointed to care for her.

The conversation did not exactly sparkle. In fact the only sound was the occasional scraping of silver on china. Well, it *is* difficult to talk to a statue of Venus.

The affair lasted for six, blissful months, until Jennings was forced to sell his love to pay off his debts.

A Romantic Skinful

Jamaican farmer Ralph Gunton was obsessed with the idea of marrying an English girl, but the candidates on the island were few and far between.

He wrote 'I'm lonely. If a pretty, domesticated girl finds this she will find me at . . . .' and pushed the bit of paper into a banana.

The melancholic missive touched the heart of an English girl who was about to bite into the yellow fruit when her eyes spotted the note.

She replied for a joke . . . and married the farmer a few months later.

To Have and to Hold

The bride walked down the aisle to the altar where her handsome groom awaited her. They were both (as were all the guests) quite naked.

They were joined in holy matrimony by the vicar who was clad only in a loin cloth.

Round the church were models of triceratops, brontosauri and other prehistoric reptiles.

'We wanted to make sure that our wedding day was a little different,' the happy couple explained.

A little?

Mounting Debts

A dashing cavalry Captain was so besotted by his beloved that in order to impress her he set spurs to his horse – and jumped over a bridge into the roaring waters of the German River Elbe.

He emerged, dripping wet, helped his horse to the banks and rode into town. Once there he headed straight for the Casino, rode up the steps into the chandelier-lit chamber, played a little roulette, won a lot at *pontoon* and left – without once dismounting.

Vaughan More Husband

Theresa Vaughan extracted her revenge on men in a most unusual way after her husband deserted her.

She travelled through Europe, across Africa and down to the Cape. When she arrived back in Britain she went up to Scotland for a few months and then to Wales.

She never stayed at the same place twice and never remained there for more than a week or two – just long enough to trap some poor unsuspecting male into marriage – 61 in all.

In the Red Corner

Appropriately enough, Derek Forbes was a *scrap* metal worker, for he liked nothing better than a couple of rounds of boxing with his young bride.

The young wife withstood this eccentric behaviour for three weeks before Derek packed a punch once too often and she packed her bags and left him.

EXTREME CASES

**Obsessives, fanatics, and their
far- fetched habits.**

Cue E.D.

Duelling was Brian Maguire's *raison d'être*. He was challenged
to defend his honour for the first time in India by a certain
Captain Thurling. Thurling had appeared at the appointed spot
armed with a magnificent sword: Brian defended himself with a
billiard cue and somehow managed to inflict a fatal injury on his
opponent!

From then on he was hooked.

Undeterred by the lack of Irishmen willing to defend their
honour, Maguire took to hanging out of the windows of his
house, throwing dirt on anyone who passed by. The dirt was
followed by an accurately aimed spit which usually caught the
unfortunate pedestrian smack in the eye, as he looked upwards.

Very few, so assaulted, could resist Maguire's challenge to
settle the matter honourably, but none of his many fights gave
him the same satisfaction as the first.

Smashing Screentest

The batty belief that wind resistance was the curse of modern
civilization was taken to eccentric extremes by one Irish earl.

He became convinced as he was driving along one day that
his new car could go much faster if he removed the front
windscreen and back window.

Not a man to rationalize his idiotic impulses, he brought the
car to a screeching halt beside a gang of labourers and
borrowed one of their hammers.

Within a few seconds, the offending glass was in
smithereens, the hammer had been returned to the astonished
workmen and the earl was on his way, as happy as a sandboy.

What's That Ear

A London man managed to control his odd tastes most of the time, but occasionally he had to give in to temptation.

He loved biting people's ears – as the policeman who tried to arrest him for suspicious behaviour one night found out, when the aural-compulsive locked on the officer's lobe, and refused to let go until passers-by came to the rescue.

Taken at Their Word

A Middlesborough woman did everything quite literally. If she was asked to run an errand – she ran. When told to take her time, she took her pulse: but she surpassed herself one night when a television announcer asked viewers to send in questions 'in a nutshell'.

She carefully took a kernel out of a walnut, put her brief question inside and sent it off.

Nuts.

Penguin Toed

Vincent Astor was obsessed with penguins. He collected live ones, of course, but he also had penguins printed on his custom-made cigarettes.

The cylinder cap of his car sported a statue of a penguin instead of the more usual flying lady. Clocks in his house, bookends, doorsteps – everything was shaped like a penguin.

His reason for this flight of fancy?

'Because they have feet like mine.'

Bridge That Gap

Joshua Norton disapproved of the way that America was, it seemed to him, drifting towards disaster in the 1850s. He decided that what was needed was a return to autocratic monarchy. Ever practical, he immediately declared himself Emperor of the United States.

For 21 years he strutted around San Francisco issuing royal edicts, insisting that he be called 'Your Majesty' and collecting 25 cents tax from shopkeepers and friends who indulged his fantasies.

To his credit, he did advocate building a bridge across the bay, but he never lived to see it. He died in 1880 in the street, wearing his full court uniform.

10,000 San Franciscans came to his funeral – a fitting tribute to the 'man who would be king'.

A Very Private Person

One famous scientist was so shy that he found it difficult to speak to his servants.

As a consequence, every door in his house was fitted with a letter box. He wrote down his instructions for the day and posted them through his housekeeper's door. Any problems were referred to him in a similar way.

In the Name of God

Terrified of the pleasures of the flesh, Onegus, an Irish saint, scourged himself constantly and recited the complete psalms of David every day — standing in a cask of cold water with a rope around his neck!

Bathed in Blankets

Scots poet William Wilkie was always reluctant to accept invitations to spend a night anywhere. He knew that his hostesses would insist on putting clean sheets on his bed – and he loathed them.

Any bed linen was immediately removed and Wilkie snuggled down under his own blankets – all twenty-four of them.

98.6°F Constant

Good health could only be maintained if the body is kept at a constant temperature – regardless of the weather. That was the crazy creed of Sir Tatton Sykes.

Little wonder that local schoolchildren followed him wherever he went. He was always wearing at least five overcoats, each one cut to fit snugly over the others, when he went out of doors. As the temperature rose, he discarded them, one after another, as a snake sheds its skin.

He was far too preoccupied to pick them up, relying instead on the honesty of the children who were rewarded with a shilling for each coat they returned to the Hall.

A Drastic Cure

Jack Mytton did nothing by half-measures. It was typical of his extraordinary and excessive enthusiasm that when he decided to shock himself out of an attack of hiccups he did so by setting fire to his nightshirt!

Bowled Out

The ambition of one eccentric scientist was to sample every drug
in the *Pharmacopeia*, the pharmacist's handbook, beginning
with the As and dosing himself with each narcotic until he
arrived at the Zs, assuming that their combined effect would not
prove fatal.

All went well at first. He dosed himself through the As and
noted the results in his journal. The B drugs were also dealt with
quite satisfactorily.

Not so the Cs. A large dose of caster oil had such a strong
effect that the scientist ran out of enthusiasm for his project and
abandoned it, a lighter but sadder man.

Booked for Theft

When police raided a Parisian man's house they found books
everywhere – piled up in the parlour, in the bathroom and hall,
scattered all over the dining room and stuffed into every
cupboard in the house. Every one was in perfect condition.

The man was arrested on a charge of shoplifting.

'Ordinarily,' he said in court, 'books never enter my head: but
as soon as I see a bookshop I cannot resist the impulse to steal
some.'

He never read them – or even opened them. He was just a
literary magpie with an incurable urge to amass volumes of
volumes.

A Slippery Character

New York girls of 1913 had to climb the stairs very warily when the phantom slipper snatcher was on the loose.

His trick was to follow women up the steps of the subway and catch hold of their shoes when they lifted their feet. Then the elusive character would run off through the rush hour crowds whooping gleefully and clutching his trophy to his breast.

He was never caught.

Any Colour – As Long As It's White

It is surely impossible for a farmer to keep himself spotlessly clean all day. Any farmer who wore light-coloured clothing while working must be mad.

BUT, Robert Cook, a seventeenth-century Irishman, insisted that everything that he wore was white; his underclothes, nightclothes, shirts, suits, coats and hats.

Not only was he always dressed in pure white, but the cows in his fields were white and so, too, were his horses.

Cook never ate meat and could not stand the thought of anyone else eating it. He took his vegetarianism to such an extreme that a fox which attacked his poultry was lectured by the farmer on the evils of eating meat, and then released. History does not tell us if the fox changed his ways, but Cook stayed true to his obsession for white right to the end. And when he was laid in his coffin, guess what colour his shroud was!

Oh To Be in England

One wealthy Indian Maharajah took his love of England to excess.

Not only was his palace an exact replica of the Victoria and Albert Museum, but it contained a roller-skating rink modelled on the one at Alexandra Palace.

His guests skated round and round to the sound of a band playing selections from *The Mikado* and other Gilbert and Sullivan gems, and when they were hungry, the palace servants dished up Brown Windsor Soup and Bread and Butter Pudding.

Bomb Mots

Otto Gardiner firmly believed that when the Germans bombed Somerset during World War II they would use old-fashioned Zeppelins with the bombs hung from the undercarriage on bits of string.

He was determined that when they flew over his estate in the West Country they should be discouraged from cutting the string. Accordingly, he ordered that his beautiful woods be cut in the shape of a Swastika, quite convinced that the Luftwaffe pilots would fly over and drop their bombs on the neighbouring grounds of Pixton where the owner had designed the park in the shape of a Union Jack.

Well Ahead of His Time

Lytton Strachey's uncle resided in India for five years and for some reason took it into his head that the only accurate clocks in the world were those in Calcutta.

So strong was this belief that when he returned to England he kept his watch and the clocks in his home on Calcutta time – six hours ahead of Greenwich Mean Time.

For 56 years he would rise in the middle of the night and go back to bed when tea was being served.

A Labour of Love

A Taiwanese actress was so involved in her work that during a performance of a harvest thanksgiving opera, *Little Dragon*, she refused to leave the stage — despite the fact that she had gone into labour. She at length gave birth to her child before the eyes of the astonished audience, who thought that it was all part of the play.

The second night audience was doubtless disappointed when the performance was not repeated the following evening.

Mummy's Boy

Whatever James Lucas wanted, his adoring mother made sure he had. If he wanted to lie in bed day after day, clinging to the plates brought to him each mealtime, why shouldn't he?

Why shouldn't he curl his hair with papers when he went out in the carriage with his sisters? And, if he insisted that a manservant followed him six paces behind, carrying a green parasol, whenever he went for a walk – so be it.

When his doting mama died in 1849, James could not bear to be parted from her, so he embalmed her and kept her at home. It took the authorities three months to persuade this latter-day Oedipus that Mrs Lucas should be given a Christian burial.

The shock of the parting was too much for the man. From the day his mother was laid to rest, he never set foot outside the kitchen of their Hertfordshire manor.

He slept on a bed of ashes taken from the fire that blazed morning, noon and night. Spring, Summer, Autumn and Winter passed; and, when he died after twenty-five years of self-imposed exile, the ashes were piled half way to the ceiling.

Odd Accounts

W. C. Fields, the inimitable American comedian, was so afraid of losing money that whenever he found himself with change or notes in his pocket he would immediately open a bank account, no matter where he was.

He never used the same name twice and never made a master list. To this day, more than forty years after his death, many of his accounts are still open.

Among the names he used were Figley E. Whitesides, Ludovic Fishpond and Cholmondley Frampton-Blythe.

Enjoying the Worst of Health

Samuel Jessop shuffled and sneezed into the Lincolnshire apothecary's shop and asked for his latest prescription to be made up.

The chemist was used to the farmer's requests, for over a period of 21 years, Sam swallowed 29 pills every day – 226,933 pills in all, *and* washed them down with 40,000 bottles of medicine!

He died in 1816 at the age of 65, never having suffered a serious illness in his life.

An All Over Scrub

The great World War II anti-guerrilla military leader Orde Wingate took it into his head that bathing was bad for a person. He kept himself scrupulously clean, however, by giving himself a good scrub with his toothbrush.

Many men who called on him were somewhat startled to see the great man sitting on a stool, brushing away – completely naked.

A Finger on the Pulse

Once an hour, on the hour, Thomas Spence took his pulse. No matter where he was or what he was doing, the happy hypochondriac would stop and make sure that all was in order.

He even ordered his coachman to pull up so that his ritual examination could take place – quite oblivious to the substantial traffic jam that built up behind him.

STRANGE HABITS

Dotty dressers and their fantastic fashions.

Never Knowingly Under-Dressed

Beau Brummel asked his valet to find out who was to be seated next to him at dinner. Not because he was afraid of sitting beside an enemy, but so that he could address his companions with suitable small talk without turning his head towards them.

He was so obsessed with the perfection of his cravat that he would not move his neck in case he creased his immaculately knotted masterpiece.

If the Coat Fits

The tailors of London's Savile Row are trained never to raise an eyebrow at the sartorial foibles of their wealthy clients. A discreet cough may occasionally express disapproval.

Whoever it was who made a certain Duke's topcoats must have coughed all the way to the bank. The coats were always ordered in threes: the first to fit over the ducal dayclothes: the second to fit over the first; and the third was perfectly cut so that the bulk of the other two would not show under it!

To complete the eccentric ensemble, his trousers were secured at the bottom with a piece of string and his headgear alone could well have earned him the title of 'mad hatter' — a shining topper, two feet high.

Dressed in this weird attire the Duke set forth, hiding behind his umbrella so as not to draw attention to himself!

Sisters Under the Skin

A white sports car drove up to the door of a Los Angeles hotel and the attractive driver asked the girl waiting for a cab if she wanted a lift.

The girl climbed in and the two drove off.

The driver was wearing a bikini top and Bermuda shorts. Her hair was in rollers.

'How far are you going?' asked the passenger.

'Just to the Convent of the Sisters of the Humility of Mary,' replied the driver. 'I'm a nun there.'

How Shoddy

The generous folk of Buckinghamshire kept John Bigg well supplied with food and drink for all the thirty years he lived in a cave at Dinton.

Bigg never asked for anything – except scraps of leather, which he immediately nailed onto his faded clothes.

When he died, one of his shoes was sent to a museum in Oxford. It was made of over 1,000 scraps of hide – 'soled' for posterity.

An Odd Nightcap

When one Englishman reads in bed he wears very suitable headgear. It keeps off the flies, shades his eyes and lets the light in.

What is the magic nightcap?

A colander.

The Mermaid of Morwenstow

The rollicking reverend of Morwenstow had a distinctly
eccentric sense of humour. Perhaps his most extraordinary
exploit concerned the mysterious appearance of a local
Mermaid . . .

One night she was spotted sitting on a rock, bathed in
moonlight, combing her long hair and crooning softly to herself.

The next night she was there again. Every man, woman and
child in the tiny fishing village watched the salty siren admiring
herself in the mirror — except, that is, for the madcap vicar.

When the Mermaid's song changed from a sweet lullaby to a bawdy ballad, hands were clapped over the children's ears. After a rousing rendition of *God Save the Queen*, the sea creature slipped off the rock and disappeared beneath the waves.

The mystery might never have been explained had not a sharp-eyed schoolboy identified the 'Mermaid' as the mad minister himself, whom he had seen slipping ashore, his legs swathed in shiny oilskins, seaweed dripping round his head and a broad grin on his face.

No doubt he claimed he had been looking for lost soles!

A Colourful Outfit

Black breeches, white stockings and a sober coat were *de rigeur* for anyone invited to appear at court by King George III.

Mr Hirst, however, had been flying in the face of convention all his life and saw no reason to change at this stage in his life.

Heads certainly turned at St James's Palace when he made his dramatic entrance. His lambskin cap was about ten feet in circumference, his otter-skinned coat lined with dazzling scarlet flannel and his waistcoat made of drake's feathers.

His patchwork breeches stopped where the red and white stockings began and his shoes were adorned with silver buckles so that they were in danger of knocking fellow courtiers off their feet.

Fortunately for Hirst, His Majesty *was* amused, chuckling over his subject's 'straordinary sartorial taste'.

A Daffy Doctor

A curious case of surgical dressing occurred when Doctor Zaharin was summoned to attend Alexander III of Russia in his last illness.

The said medico arrived at the palace door in his carriage swathed in furs. He then proceeded to drop his fur wrap on the hall floor, his overcoat in the next room, his hat in the next and so on through the ten royal antechambers until he arrived at the dying Czar's bedside in ordinary indoor clothes.

The consultation over, he progressed back through the royal antechambers picking up and putting on his clothes as he went, until he was finally warmly wrapped up against the elements when he got back to his carriage.

A Proper Queen

When Queen Anne appointed her cousin, Lord Cornbury, to the Governor-Generalship of her American colonies she little realized that he would take his duties as her representative quite so literally. He stunned New Yorkers and members of the Diplomatic Corps by appearing at official receptions wearing hooped gowns, a wig, elegant head-dresses and carrying a fan.

'One wouldn't mind,' one woman was heard to say. 'But he is such a large man.'

Not Quite the Full Shilling

Hot pants have been banned from the Royal Enclosure at Ascot for many years. Ladies' hats must now cover the crown. (How will the Queen manage?) Men must wear morning suits or uniforms. But nothing so far has managed to suppress the outrageous hats worn by Mrs Gertrude Shilling.

Over the years, she has graced the Royal Enclosure with six-foot-wide flower-decked extravaganzas; enormous shiny black silk skyscrapers have almost obscured the horses from the race-goers' binoculars; model coronation coaches, song birds, feathers, Union Jacks — you name it, it's been atop Mrs Shilling's pretty head.

Of course, off course, she's the mother of fashionable milliner David Shilling and is doing what any loving mother would do to promote her son's business; but even so, one feels that she's gone quite a bit over the topper.

What an Order

Polite patrons in a Bath coffee house were amazed when
William Cussans, a notable eighteenth century eccentric, called
for a pitcher of water and, when it was brought, poured it over
himself.

He sat there, the water running off him, and ordered his
lunch – a pint of vinegar and some barley sugar.

His oddity was confirmed when he next proceeded to take six
shirts out of his bag and put them on *over* his coat. He then told
the landlord that he would return for supper – a dish of fried
milestones.

A Bleeding Shame

The First World War need never have happened if Archduke
Francis Ferdinand, whose assassination sparked off the whole
thing, had not been so pernickety about his clothes.

He was so determined that there should be no creases in his
uniforms that he had himself sewn into them before each public
appearance.

The stitching was so strong on that fateful day in Sarajevo
that the Archduke bled to death before a pair of scissors could
be found to cut his clothes off and stem the bleeding.

The Naked Dueller

One young buck liked nothing better than settling a matter of honour in the traditional way.

His opponents were staggered whenever he arrived to fight, for he removed his greatcoat and boots, gave them to his second and faced his rival completely naked.

His nudity was necessary, for he believed that clothes were frightfully septic, and if he was unlucky enough to be hit by a bullet, the chances of infection would be greatly increased if as much as a fragment of material was lodged in his body.

Off his Pterodactyl

Ramblers making the most of the fine weather on the Berkshire Downs could well have been forgiven for thinking that they had strolled into a time warp.

A giant shape swooped down out of nowhere, flew above their bemused heads for a minute or two, before flapping its mighty wings and disappearing over the horizon.

Was it a bird? Was it Superman? No. It was the incredibly lifelike creation of a well-known author whose hobby is making remote-controlled prehistoric monsters and springing them on unwary walkers, causing panic to swell in their healthy hearts.

Mr . . . also has plans to enliven Royal Ascot, the highlight of the summer Racing Calendar. He intends to persuade his high-spirited girlfriend to wear a remote-controlled hat shaped like a prehistoric bird into the Royal Enclosure.

What will Her Majesty say when the lavishly decorated, wide-brimmed headgear zooms across the hallowed turf? One thinks that Mr . . . will count himself lucky if he is not warned off for life.

Three Months' Worth

Eccentric millionaire Perry Ball sauntered into a Savile Row tailor and asked for some outfits to be made to see him through the winter.

Not a person to appear twice in the same clothes, Perry ordered 500 suits, jackets, sweaters, hats and the other bare essentials necessary for a man who changed his clothes six times every day.

The £35,000 invoice (£250,000 allowing for inflation) was paid in cash.

Cultural Craziness

Glyndbourne, where opera lovers feast on *Fidelio* and Fortnum's hampers, was founded by John Christie, one of the most unconventional men of his time.

When he took it into his head to wear *lederhosen*, in 1933, all his guests were expected to wear them too.

He owned almost 200 handkerchiefs, 110 shirts, 132 pairs of socks – but only one pair of battered shoes. These were plimsolls that he wore all the time – even with formal evening dress.

His friends never knew what to expect, but even those who knew him best were astonished when he turned round to the Queen and asked 'Is it straight, Ma'am?'

He was not referring to his tie – but to his glass eye that he had just popped back in place during dinner one night.

The White Man Cometh

A nineteenth-century African chief set out one day to meet the distinguished Englishman who was exploring his tribal lands.

He wanted to impress the white man so he dressed himself in his full regalia – ostrich-feather cloak, elaborate headdress and painted face.

He stopped in his tracks when he saw the intrepid visitor approaching. He was sitting astride an ox, wearing full hunting pink. An ear trumpet was held to his left ear and he was surveying the scene with a pair of opera glasses.

The African must have wondered who was civilizing whom!

If the Cap Fits

Customers in a smart London department store were astonished one day by a certain gentleman's behaviour. He sat in front of a gilt mirror amid startled assistants and fashionably dressed women in the millinery department, trying on hats. Frothy little confections, fetching feathered numbers, wide-brimmed picture hats were all plonked on top of his shining pate, until he at last decided on a rather smart little pill-box in a pretty shade of grey.

   He wasn't a frustrated fetishist or troubled transvestite. He always liked to surprise his wife on her birthday with an Easter bonnet and he reckoned if it suited him it would suit her, too.

The Mad Hatter

The moment the clock struck seven, a manservant unscrewed the knocker from Richard Kirwan's front door. Any latecomers to his twice weekly soirées could rap their fists on the heavy oak until blood ran from their knuckles – no one was admitted after seven.

Inside, it was a different matter. The atmosphere was friendly and warm – the friendliness encouraged by the dazzling conversation, the warmth created by the flames of the roaring fire that blazed in the fireplace, no matter how warm the weather.

In front of the fire sat the host, reclining on a sofa, wearing not one, but two overcoats and his hat.

He refused to remove his hat no matter where he was. Perhaps he was afraid that the tame eagle that was always perched on his shoulder might revert to the wild and peck his bald pate.

After two hours, Kirwan stood up and removed his shoes and buckles, leaving his guests in no doubt that it was time for them to go. A last flap of the eagle's wings soon saw any lingerers off the premises and the exceptional host – plus hat – could retire to bed.

Saddle Sore

Lord Barrymore, one-time boon companion of the Prince of Wales, loved riding but loathed riding gear. Not for him the black, polished boots, white breeches and well-tailored coats of his fellows. He rode out into the world as he had come into it – starkers.

DEAD ODD

**Weird wills, funny funerals and
dotty demises.**

Well Preserved

Martin Butcher could not bear to have his dead wife buried. He had her embalmed and personally injected some carmine dye into her veins to give her dead skin a rosy flush. He also selected the glass eyes that were to be used, and dressed her himself in her favourite lace gown.

The mummy of his children was then laid to rest in a glass-topped case in the parlour, where Martin's grieving eyes could admire his handicraft.

Only Martin's eyes were not grieving. They were quite dry. A clause in his marriage agreement had given him the interest in his wife's not inconsiderable fortune 'as long as she is above the ground'.

Martin was not going to give up his income by having his wife buried *underground*. There was nothing the trustees of the late Mrs Butcher could do. She lay, like Sleeping Beauty, in her transparent coffin, and Martin continued to collect for several months, until he was finally persuaded to bury the casket.

A Grave Injustice

Robert Terrell went through the latter years of his life with a heavy burden on his shoulders — his mother's tombstone.

It was the only way he could prove that he was entitled to security benefits, for he had lost his birth certificate, and as the stone said that his mother died in 1901, he had to be at least 62 in 1963 when he started to claim his pension . . . and his concessionary travel . . . and the other freebies enjoyed by America's senior citizens.

Black Humour

Dorothea Herbert went into the deepest mourning when her husband died. All her servants were dressed in black – even the white horse in the stables was dyed black.

She then proceeded to paint every room and door-frame the same colour and decided that all the furniture be painted black, too.

The upholsterer was so appalled at the prospect when he came to her sombre house to discuss the matter that he refused to carry out the work.

Dorothea ordered a maid to lock him up until he changed his mind. Fortunately he managed to escape both from captivity and from the odious commission.

A Funny Funeral

Three thousand people turned up to Tim Dexter's funeral. His black-dressed servants ushered them into the huge mansion where Tim had died and served drinks while the mourners waited for the obsequies to begin.

With tongues loosened by a liberal lashing of whisky, the conversation rose to a crescendo and then stopped suddenly when Tim appeared amongst them – large as life and twice as kicking.

He explained to his astonished friends (and the many joyriders who had heard the party in full swing) that he wanted to see what his funeral would be like.

He was tempting fate, for he died laughing before he was 60.

Prepared for the End

Old John was laid in his coffin. No one wept. Not a lump came to a throat as the box was carried out.

Had John been a bad master or cruel father? No! He was a popular local figure around Letchworth. It was simply that the old man enjoyed being carried round his garden in an open coffin.

As he explained to one astonished acquaintance who caught him in his macabre exercise, 'I'm getting ready'.

A Clean Grave

There are many stories of men and women becoming so attached to their pets that they organize lavish funerals for them – but one Scottish woman outdid them all.

She planted a beautiful rose bush above her interred vacuum cleaner.

Poor sucker.

Alas, Poor Yorick

Long after his life had ended, John Reed achieved his life-long ambition. Having lost his heart to the theatre, he left his head to it in his will.

'My head be separated from my body immediately after my death, the latter to be buried in a grave, the former duly macerated and prepared to be brought to the theatre . . . and to be employed to represent the skull of Yorick.'

No one who worked in the Philadelphia theatre where John was employed as a gas lighter had realized that he carried such a torch for the acting profession, but the would-be thespian's burning ambition was eventually realized.

Play Those Skins Man

When S. Sanborn of Massachusetts bequeathed his body to medical science he was quite aware that the researchers would have little use for his skin.

Ever ingenious, he left it to a friend, one Warren Simpson, on the condition that he had it made into two drumheads, one inscribed with Alexander Pope's Universal Prayer, the other with the Declaration of Independence.

Every year on June 17, Simpson was directed to take the drums to the top of Bunker Hill and beat *Yankee Doodle Dandy* on them.

Mr Simpson was sufficiently fond of his dead friend – and sufficiently patriotic – to carry out these instructions every year until he died.

A Slip of the Pen

The two nurses told the patient who was about to die that they could not find any writing paper for him to write his will on.

Not a man to take such an inconvenience lying down, George Hazeltine dictated his last wishes to one of his devoted Nightingales, who took them down on her petticoat.

Unfortunately, the old saying 'where there's a will there's a way' was not proved to be true on this occasion, as the makeshift will was found to be illegal.

No one Knows Y

The Rev John Gwyon, rector of Bisley, left almost £10,000 when he died. His executors were directed at first to pay off any outstanding debts. Then with the money left over, they were to provide a well-known brand of men's underwear for all the boys in his parish.

Snookered

An Australian snooker player was determined to invent a new trick shot that would take his name into the record books along with Joe Davies, 'Hurricane' Higgins and his other heroes.

He attached helium-filled balloons to his wrists and had himself suspended over the table, his legs tied to the rafters. The crowd held its breath as he prepared to make his first shot in this state of suspended animation.

Unfortunately he fell head first onto the table, cracked his skull and died in hospital shortly afterwards.

A Helluva, Swelluva Party

Dallas folk look forward to the annual bash thrown by a local millionaire.

At the height of the fun they gather round him and drink his health in the best champagne. Their host never says a word.

He lies in his hermetically sealed, glass-topped coffin, a smile on his lips, happy in the knowledge that the trust fund he set up to pay for the fun is being well administered.

The Worms Would Eat Me . . .

John Farmer left instructions that on his death he was to be seated in his mausoleum, fully clothed, with a bottle of claret in one hand and a glass in the other. Broken glass was to be scattered around his feet to discourage devils from coming too near.

When asked why he did not want to be buried in the conventional manner, Farmer replied, 'The worms would eat me, the ducks would eat the worms and my family would eat the ducks. I don't want to be eaten by my relatives.'

Grave Delights

No cheeks were wetter than Jamie Duff's as the deceased was lowered into the ground. No voice was louder in the 'Amens', and no clothes were blacker than his cravat, cape and top hat.

Sometimes Jamie was acquainted with the dear departed, more often he was a complete stranger.

Hardly a citizen of Edinburgh was sent to meet his maker without Jamie leading the mourners – for well over forty years.

The Nuts of Nantwich

When the bailiffs broke into a house in Nantwich to repossess its contents they expected some opposition, but not three wailing harpies screaming, 'This is God's house. There is fire and brimstone in every room. Mother must not be touched. She is in God's hands.'

The law officers made their way into the kitchen where an old lady sat before a table spread with fruit, nuts and a pot of hot tea.

She certainly was in God's hands. The coroner at the subsequent inquest reckoned that she had been dead for at least five years!

A Grave Consultation

For 55 years Doctor Charles White visited Miss Beswick. He climbed the stairs, drew back the velvet drapes and bade 'Good morning' to his patient.

She never responded.

She had died in 1758 and left the physician £25,000 on the condition that he visited her once a year on the anniversary of her death.

He kept her mummified body in a grandfather clock in his attic, visiting it annually and enjoying the fruits of his long-dead patient's generosity.

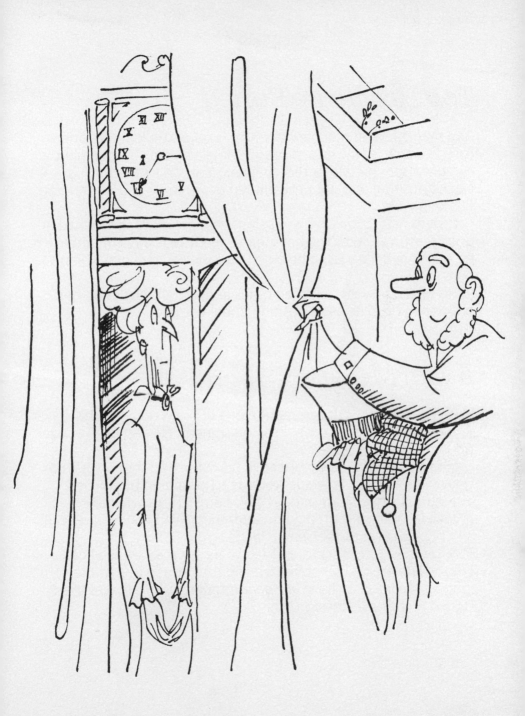

Too Lazy to be Buried

As a magistrate of much experience, François Helloin was often called upon to settle local disputes. He gladly did so — beaming benignly from his bed or reclining languidly on a silk sofa. His supine position was not necessitated by illness or injury. François was bone idle.

He left instructions in his will that when he died (and he had good reason to suppose that the sad event would occur when he was in bed) he was to be buried in a wood-lined grave, in his bed.

His oddness was confirmed by his demand that his chamber pot was to be in its usual position under the bed.

Beam Me Up

When a certain Hertfordshire farmer's will was read out, his family looked at each other in astonishment. He had been a little odd, but this . . .?

His last wish was to be placed in his coffin and then — far from going *under*ground — he desired to be hoisted up by a pulley and hung from a beam in one of his barns! Thus, when he awoke (as he anticipated doing after thirty years) he would be in a happy position to oversee his lands.

After the allotted score-and-ten years, his relieved relations cut the late great crackpot down and thus ended one of the longest recorded cases of '*suspended* animation'. He was then buried in the usual fashion.

Driven to the Grave

Sandra West was only thirty-seven when she died. She left her entire estate, £1.5 million, to her brother on condition that he followed her burial instructions to the letter.

She was to be dressed in her lace nightgown and placed sitting at the wheel of her blue 1964 Ferrari, with the seat slanted comfortably. The car was to be packed in wood, wrapped in steel and encased in concrete before being interred in the family plot.

Mrs West was duly despatched to meet her maker according to her bizarre wishes.

Just a Quick One

A London dyer was determined that a good time was going to be had by all his guests.

First of all everyone would stop off outside the Blue Boar in Westminster and drink a gallon of gin. Suitably refreshed, the party would move on to the Jolly Sawyers in Lambeth for another eight pints of mothers' ruin.

The only person who didn't drink was the host. The dyer was dead!

His funeral procession was one of the jolliest ever and, as his coffin was lowered into the ground, the merry mourners raised gin-filled glasses in a farewell toast to their host.

CREDITABLE CRANKS

**The weird and wonderful ways of
the wealthy.**

Flashy Fish

Emperor Jahamgir of India enjoyed fishing. But unlike other anglers he never killed his catch.

Instead he threaded a string of pearls through the fishes' gills and threw them back into the water.

He could well afford to create such a splash – he owned a total of 2,235,600 carats of pearls along with 931,500 carats of emeralds, 376,600 of rubies, 279,450 of diamonds and 186,300 of jade.

His contemporaries thought that he was stoned out of his mind.

The Stamp of Her Personality

Victoria-Josefa Sackville-West could have well afforded to have her servants deliver her mail by hand had she so desired. Although she was rich she saw no reason why she should waste money on postage stamps.

Instead, she cut up used stamps and pieced the unfranked portions together so that she could save a few coppers each time she posted a letter.

She didn't waste much money on writing paper either. The toilet paper in Harrods was quite serviceable and, if she ran short of that, there were always old newspapers, backs of old envelopes and other scraps that she came across.

She ruthlessly plundered hotels for the headed notepaper left for the use of guests, and she gave one friend food for thought when she scribbled a note to her on an old piece of ham. That message went unanswered. There was, the recipient said, no cure for such behaviour.

A Little Gift to the Government

Other Indian potentates impressed their guests with lavish meals served on gold and silver plates. Not the Nizam of Hyderabad.

Despite his fabulous wealth (which easily enabled him to sign a cheque for £25,000,000 as a contribution to the British Government's War Effort in 1914), all that his guests were given was a cup of tea and a biscuit. *One* cup of tea and *one* biscuit. Smokers were then given one cigarette.

When the last fag-end had been stubbed out, the visitors were ushered from the royal presence, leaving the Nizam to scrabble in the ashtrays and smoke the dog ends! Hardly surprising that he was the butt of many an unkind joke in diplomatic circles.

Jewels on Wheels

Pedestrians gawped whenever Lilian Russel, comedienne girlfriend of diamond millionaire Jim Brady, flashed by on her bicycle – for Lilian really *did* flash.

The bike was a little gift from Diamond Jim. The handlebars were inlaid with mother of pearl ('Chromium is for ordinary people.'), the wheels were studded with diamonds, sapphires, rubies and emeralds – the original be*spoke* jewellery perhaps.

Pushing the pedals of her valuable velocipede as fast as she could, Lilian cycled everywhere, quite aware of the stir she created.

When she travelled by train – her bike went too, in a specially made travelling case of the best Moroccan leather.

When her turbulent relationship with Diamond Jim eventually fell apart, Lilian could well be forgiven for thinking that she had gone through hell for leather!

One Wishes One Had Known Her

Like many wealthy Americans of the 1920s Laura Corrigan was
determined to launch herself on London Society. She gave lavish
parties and, to ensure people came, bribed them with gold
cigarette holders, diamond lighters and other little baubles.

Her butler was given instructions that anyone who called at
her house in Grosvenor Square was to be given a cocktail; a
succession of tipsy butcher's boys, chauffeurs and dressmakers
were seen to gulp down a White Lady or a Brandy Alexander

before getting back to business.

When Prince George came to dinner, she ordered that Fortnum and Mason send round not four or five of their famous hampers — but the entire stock of the famous food hall.

When His Royal Highness arrived he was greeted by the awesome sight of his hostess standing on her head, her silk knickers exposed for all to see; but such was the glorious gusto with which she entertained that he forgave her her bloomers and Laura became the toast of the town.

The Dreadful Dancers

Dan Dancer and his sister were very wealthy. They had an annual income of over £3,000 which was a considerable amount of money in the eighteenth century. They loathed spending a penny of it.

Even when Miss Dancer was dying, Dan refused to call in a doctor or to change her diet – one cold dumpling and a scrap of meat each day.

'Why should I,' he asked, 'waste my money in wickedly endeavouring to counteract the will of Providence?'

Dan was well known for his miserliness. While out walking one day he came across the rotting carcass of a dead sheep. He skinned it and had the decaying meat made into pies. The bone he gave to his dog.

He obtained fertilizer for his fields by stuffing his pockets with cow dung he found while out walking. His day was made if he came across any old bones while scavenging. Any meat on them was cooked and served for his dinner.

But even Dan surpassed himself when he received a gift of a trout stewed in claret. Unfortunately, the fish had become frozen solid during transport.

He refused to eat it, for he had a bad tooth which was aggravated by anything cold. Dental treatment was, of course, out of the question, being far too expensive. Nor did he want to spend money on having the unexpected gift heated over a fire.

He came up with his own unique solution. He sat on it until the fish had thawed out, and then ate it with much enjoyment.

Caught Short

A wealthy but scruffy tourist in Buenos Aires fell off a bus and broke his leg.

He was rushed to a nearby charity hospital where he was unable to make the staff understand that he could well afford a private room. He had to suffer the indignity of being put in a ward full of pitiful peasants and being treated as one of them.

Following the dictum, 'once bitten, twice shy', from then on he saw to it that whenever he left home he carried with him the wherewithal to pay for treatment in a decent private hospital.

A sensible precaution, you may think, but he went just a bit far — carrying wherever he went £1,000 worth each of dollars, francs, guilders, milreis, yen, zlotys, taler, pesos, marks, drachmas and pengos — plus the odd £100 note.

Cross Channel Viewing

Having made a vast fortune out of 'cat's eyes', their inventor could afford to indulge his every whim. He could have bought a Greek island, travelled the world in luxury liners and wined and dined in the plushest restaurants.

He didn't buy the island, but he did travel, wine and dine.

Every night he was driven to his local pub, where he munched his way through box after box of potato crisps washed down with Brown Ale; and, as he ate, his eyes hardly left the *three* television sets the publican had installed for him — one tuned to BBC1, another to BBC2 and the third to ITV.

Changed My Mind

Passengers on the *Aquitania* were fabulously rich – they had to be to afford the price of a cruise on the lavish ship.

Every suite and state room was adorned with copies of great paintings, including Gainsborough's *Blue Boy*. The famous masterpiece took the fancy of one multi-millionaire's wife who insisted that her adoring husband buy the original for her.

The then Duke of Westminster, who was the owner of the painting, was thunderstruck to receive an offer for it for £400,000. He accepted it and the painting was crated and sent to California.

When it arrived, the capricious woman took one look at it and said that it was a lot *greener* than the reproduction and refused to have it hung anywhere in her house.

Her husband contacted the shipping line and bought the copy for a few hundred dollars, while Gainsborough, no doubt, revolved in his grave.

Mechanical Music

The sound of 150 recorders, 150 flutes, 50 oboes, 18 trumpets, 3 drums and 2 kettledrums was music to the ears of Karl Waetzel. He played them all – at the same time.

His invention – the panomonica – is the only one-man orchestra in the world.

The Archduke Charles of Austria was entranced by it and paid Karl a large sum of money for the solo band.

His courtiers were not so enthralled – Charles used the mad machine to shut them up whenever they were making too much noise.

She's Such a Pet

A certain vet was called to examine and treat a rather pampered pug belonging to an old lady whose parsimony was legendary.

As he was about to leave, the penny-pinching heiress asked him if he would mind looking at another patient upstairs.

She led the way to the servants' quarters, where one of her maids was sick in bed.

'You don't mind, do you?' the old lady asked quite disarmingly. 'Doctors are such a ridiculous waste of money!'

Looking After the Pennies

With an inheritance of £250,000 (a vast amount of money in the eighteenth century) the son of a Southwark brewer could well afford to indulge his every whim.

Why should such riches stop him going to bed as soon as it got dark so as to save on candles? Why should there be a fire in the grate no matter how cold it was?

The old beggar's wig that he found in a hedge one day was still serviceable, so why shouldn't he wear it for a week or two?

There's nothing wrong with a few maggots, is there? And so what if the roof leaks? There's always another corner where you can shelter.

Why pay tolls if by going a few miles out of your way they can be avoided? And if the road surface wears out the horse's hooves, what's wrong with riding along the grass verge.

Hardly surprising that when he died in 1789, the £250,000 had grown to a cool million!

Soft in the Head

American millionaire, Willie Walter, was so convinced that his deteriorating sight had been caused by bumping his head on the roof of his car that he had a special one made.

The new automobile was tall enough for him to stand up in and, as his chauffeur drove through the uptown traffic, Willie stood hanging on to a leather strap attached to the roof – for all the world like an office-worker in a rush hour subway!

A Glittering Gozunder

One fabulously wealthy American studded everything in his house with precious stones. Even the chamber utensil under his bed was covered in diamonds and rubies.

Quite fabulously potty.

Fore and Daft

It cost financial wizard Ned Green one million dollars to buy the *United States*. Not the country, the yacht that sailed on the Great Lakes.

It wasn't large enough for the grand ideas of the Colonel of Wall Street, so he had it cut in half and a new piece was fitted in the middle. Nor was one captain enough for Ned.

He appointed two – one for each end – but fortunately neither had to try to exert his authority over the other, for the eccentrically extended ship sank before its maiden voyage.

The Power of Money

The new house that one American millionaire bought had just one little thing wrong with it. There were rooms for only fifteen servants – at least another forty were needed.

She ordered her architect to pull the whole place down and build a new house from scratch to be ready by the following season. Armies of workmen toiled through the winter and the house was finished on time.

'Do you like it, ma'am?' the anxious architect asked, after its owner had finished inspecting it.

'It's still too small. Pull it down and start again,' was the only reply.

An Expensive Little Hobby

Howard Hughes, the eccentric millionaire, liked to 'dabble' in aviation. He once spent $50,000,000 (a quarter of a million pounds at the then exchange rate) to develop the 'Hercules' – a vast, eight-engined flying boat designed to carry 700 passengers.

Hughes personally took the controls of the prototype on its flight and flew it for one mile. Apparently unimpressed by its performance, he lost interest in the project, preferring to concentrate on a long-range reconnaissance 'plane which unfortunately crashed on its maiden flight – again with Hughes in the cockpit.

He did however, have one more fortunate engineering venture: the bra he designed to emphasise film star Jane Russell's well-endowed chest was an outstanding success.

Waste Not, Want Not

The niece of a well-known millionairess was pleasantly surprised to be asked to tea by her aunt.

The tray was brought in by the housemaid – silver tea pot, hot water jug, sugar and cucumber sandwiches.

'You don't take milk, do you dear?' the old lady asked, and when the answer was 'yes', she turned to the maid and said, 'Emily, if the cat has left any milk, bring it up please.'

Not that the cat was pampered in any way. It suffered from the household economies, too. When its mistress found a dead sparrow in Hyde Park, she put it in her handbag and carried it home, where she ordered the staff to 'discommand the cat's meat' and serve the deceased bird to her pet mog.

No Change

An old Irishman was very wealthy, but his riches did not prevent him from collecting old candle wax wherever he happened to be, melting it down and selling remoulded candles for a considerable profit.

Nor did all his money give him an appetite for fine food. He dined every day on a halfpenny's worth of bread and milk, fetched for him by an old servant woman.

The tragic day came when the old woman slipped and broke her leg, letting her master's lunch roll into the street.

'Where's the jug, Katie?' he asked kindly when he visited her in hospital.

'Smashed,' she sobbed.

'And the bread?'

'In the gutter.'

Her employer nodded sympathetically. Then: 'Where's my halfpenny change . . .?' A classic case of taking care of the pennies.

Sale or Return

Despite her considerable wealth, Venetia James liked to buy everything on a sale or return basis – even her butcher meat! Anything that was unused was sent back to the shop and credited to her account.

Venetia always contrived to ensure that there was something to go back. She could stretch a seemingly small joint to amazing lengths, but she surpassed herself one day when she managed to carve a small chicken into ten portions.

Her butler understood the odd message that she passed to him on a piece of paper – DCSC: don't cut second chicken.

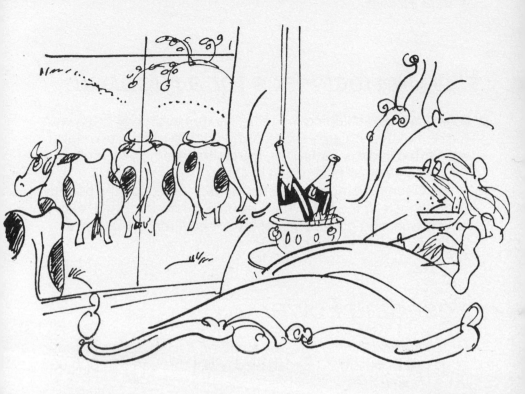

A Lot of Hot Air

Fresh air and methane gas are vital to one's health. That was the firm belief of one elderly autocrat. She was wealthy enough to insist that wherever she stayed she was put in a ground floor bedroom, overlooking a field full of cows.

When she retired for the evening, orders were issued that the animals were to be tethered, their heads facing away from the house, their rear ends pointing towards the old lady's bedroom so that any wind that they broke while she was sleeping was aimed straight at her!

It must have worked, for she lived until she was 84; or maybe the pint of milk and two bottles of Krug champagne that she drank every day for the last year of her life had something to do with her longevity.

The Perfect Place for a Highball

A certain Greek shipping magnate's luxury yacht was fitted with the best of everything – El Grecos hung on the walls, gold taps were fitted in every bathroom, the clothes worn by the dolls in the nursery had all been made by Dior.

The owner's flamboyant tastes perhaps exceeded the bounds of good taste in the bar, where, as he gleefully informed many an unsuspecting guest, the stools were covered with whales' testicles.

Spending Power

James Gordon Bennet had one ambition – to spend his billions as quickly as possible. He managed to get through £25,000,000 in his lifetime. He:

tipped the guard on the prestigious locomotive, the *Train Bleu*, £10,000;

spent £150,000 on a pair of gilt statues to sit on top of his office headquarters;

bought a silver-topped desk for £10,000 and never used it;

designed a new skyscraper with a magnificent penthouse office for himself – costing many, many millions of dollars.

He decided that he ought to visit his splendid new office building and penthouse, so he sailed his yacht into New York harbour and jumped into a cab to take him to Manhattan.

On the way he stopped off at his club and ordered his favourite lunch – lamb chops. They arrived very over-cooked. Bennet stormed out of the club, back to his yacht and sailed away. He never returned to New York again and his multi-million dollar office-block remained unused.